# The Child
## Within the LOTUS

MARGARET STEPHENSON MEERE

# The Child
## within the LOTUS

### HUMAN BEHAVIOUR FROM BIRTH

## MARGARET STEPHENSON MEERE

ROCKPOOL
PUBLISHING

A Rockpool book
Published by Rockpool Publishing
24 Constitution Road, Dulwich Hill, NSW 2023, Australia
www.rockpoolpublishing.com.au

First published in 2009
Copyright © Margaret Stephenson Meere, 2009

National Library of Australia
Cataloguing-in-Publication entry


Stephenson-Meere, Margaret.
The child within the lotus / Margaret Stephenson Meere.
9781921295164 (pbk.)
A823.4

Tom Chetwynd, *A Dictionary of symbols* reprinted by
permission of Harper Collins Publishers Ltd © Tom Chetwynd, 1982

Every effort has been made to identify copyright holders of extracts in this book. The publishers
would be pleased to hear from any copyright holders who have not been acknowledged.

Edited by Gabiann Marin
Cover and internal design by Seymour Designs
Illustrations by diacriTech, India
Typeset by J&M Typesetting
Printed and bound by KHL Printing Co. Pte Ltd in Singapore

10 9 8 7 6 5 4 3 2 1

The information provided in this book is intended for general information and guidance only,
and should not be used as a substitute for consulting a qualified health practitioner. Neither
the author nor the publisher can accept responsibility for any problems arising out of the
contents of this book.

*This book is dedicated to the memory of my parents*
*Charles and Anne Meere,*
*who gave me their wisdom*
*and my childhood,*

*and to*
*Gary Lewin,*
*who gave me the love and support*
*needed for its creation.*

# CONTENTS

# SECTION III – Self-responsibility

# SECTION IV – Self-reflection

# EPILOGUE

# APPENDICES

*It is from the flower that the child is born.*
*The child within the lotus: the true centre of life from*
*which the pattern of life, like the pattern of the lotus,*
*can be discerned. All the promise and potential within*
*the individual, all the possibilities for change, development*
*and transformation within the psyche are summed*
*up in the image of the child.*

TOM CHETWYND  *A DICTIONARY OF SYMBOLS*

# Introduction

One day I was clearing out a cupboard and I came across a book that I had purchased and read more that ten years earlier – Hiroshi Motoyama's *Theories of the Chakras: Bridge to Higher Consciousness*. As I held this book in my hand, it opened to a colour plate of a chakra and I was amazed to find that what I was looking at was a newborn child. I knew then, in that brief moment of epiphany, that my first book, *Baby's First 100 Days*, had been about the awakening of the first energy centre.

I was not very knowledgeable in this area of spirituality and even though I knew deep within me that I had stumbled upon a universal truth, I realised that I had a lot more learning to do. So for a year I undertook a formal study of spiritual metaphysics and grew more confident in my belief. I knew even less about the lotus, but now one breathes in my balcony pond and is a constant source of observation, learning, joy and meditative contemplation. Even in winter dormancy, it lies in mystery within its muddy subconscious, waiting for the springtime to rise through the water with new growth.

Subsequently the format of this book began a metamorphosis and it is now a book about human spiritual development as well as the practical aspects of the development of human behaviour. It is a book about a child, beginning from the time before he or she is born. This book is the blending of current western knowledge and ancient eastern wisdom. It takes into account the anatomy of growth, both physical and subtle, for we are more than just the fleshy visible parts of our physical body, we are also contained within our invisible anatomy – the emotional, mental and spiritual energies that cannot be seen by the naked eye.

When we are born we are in a state of unity with all things. This state is our spiritual core. We trust life implicitly, not fearing that we can be dropped from a great height, or that the next meal might not be available for us; or that there is 'not enough'. For our first 100 days of life we are part of being connected. Then, as we mature and grow into our second 100 days, we begin to learn of life's dualities.

We yearn to connect with the child within us, and with its innocence which we can remember on a deep 'spiritual' level from our very early days after birth. This memory is contained within every cell of our body.

Spirituality grows out of the process of mental development rather than dogma. So many special areas of life as an individual human being influence this process. Our spiritual path is a personal choice and it is influenced by our mental disposition, our temperament, our belief systems, our family, our education and our cultural background. Initially it develops out of desire and once we have taken our first few steps of exploration, life conspires to make it happen for us. Doors and windows of opportunity open and they are always perfect for what we need to learn at that specific time in our life. Often we can view these learning experiences as unfortunate or negative aspects of our life, but in time and in retrospect we often find the seed of a new life experience in the shell of that old part of us.

Spiritual growth is a journey. The path that we decide to tread is usually one that is less travelled. However, in a new millennium there are signs of change, with many individuals choosing to avoid materialism and to embrace a new spirituality and to trust their process within it.

The concept of God, as written in this book, is one that describes a force that is contained within each individual and is used to embrace the part of the personal and broader landscape that forms our existence and the existence of all things. The concept of God can only ever be a personal one which comes from our own understanding of the world and our ability to grow spiritually.

In this book are some keys to help a child unlock his potential spiritual growth which we, as parent, guardian and nurturer, are in a unique position to provide.

The newborn child is a very spiritual being. He lives in the 'now', he is the most honest that he will ever be in his whole life, he is extremely intuitive and he emanates a presence which is so powerful that it can draw us into its light. The newborn child *is* the centre of the Universe, the godhead at the centre of all things, *the child within the lotus*.

This is a book about aspects of human growth and behaviour, from the time in the womb to the mature years of life. It has an emphasis on the spiritual aspects of growth, but rather than being esoteric it is presented in a language that I hope can be appreciated by all readers. Often the concept of spirituality is confused with religion, but while spirituality is part of the individual and is internalised, religion belongs to the masses and is external to the individual. We express our spirituality in our journey through life. All of us have the capacity to modify our own behaviour and it is through this process that our spirituality evolves and grows. For many it becomes a conscious act, a decision to change the way that we see and exist within our world. In this way it is a revolution. We search out new ways or paths.

In the western world, societies have come to rely strongly, and sometimes exclusively, on scientific proof. However the wisdom and writings of ancient Greek and eastern philosophers are as relevant to life today as they were in their own times. These philosophers did not have scientific proof of their theories about humans and their universe; they had a solid understanding that just because something cannot be fully validated, this lack of proof does not negate its existence.

Writing this book has been a rich and rewarding journey for me. I have learnt through working alongside and counselling new parents that there is a need to articulate the spiritual journey that comes with the birthing process, parenting and the understanding of our child.

In modern societies we are losing touch with our spiritual nature and I believe that this is leading to a conflict of belief systems and a disruption of cultures. Our children are growing up within this confusion. It is through us, as adults, that children need the guidance and nurturing that is required for them to continue to live the spiritual life in a material world. To bring peace to all peoples we all need to develop true love and gratitude for what life gives us. It is the only way that we can begin to heal our own inner child, to preserve the wholeness of our children and to develop the special love and compassion that is needed to heal our planet.

My vision for this book is that it can help us with this healing.

# How to use this book

The growth and development of an infant is incredibly rapid and it is in these very early years of childhood that many, and probably most, of our behavioural patterns are laid down. We all have begun from a germination of hope and love – none of us escaped the wonder, beauty and trauma of being a child and it is from those early childhood years that we have become the individuals we are today.

This is, therefore, a book for everyone, whether you are parenting a little child, considering having a child, or even thinking about your own childhood and wanting to parent your own personal development.

This book is designed in sections to lead the reader through the developmental stages of human behaviour. When we gain an understanding of what is normal age-appropriate behaviour then we are more able to make intuitive decisions about how to nurture a child.

The first two sections of the book, from Chapter 1 to Chapter 5, describes the first five chakras. Each of these chapters covers a 100-day period until the child is about 18 months of age, when a child develops a greater capacity for language. Until oral language or speech begins to develop, understanding the behaviour of a child can be a bit of a mystery for a new parent, so the first five sections contain a practical component dealing with the basics of sleeping and feeding for your guidance. Chapter 1 introduces the child's early development of sense of *self*.

Chapter 5 deals more with the development of speech and the child's growing capacity for *self-control*.

The third section of the book, the sixth chakra or the third eye, discusses the child of about eight years – the age of consciousness, when a child develops a capacity for complex and rational thinking. This may seem like a massive jump from two to eight years, but it is included because this age marks a turning point in how we can relate to our child and also in how we can understand their changing thinking patterns. This child is beginning middle childhood – the bridge from early childhood to adolescence when she will begin to move away from the protection of family towards a new *self-responsibility*.

The fourth section contains the seventh chapter, the seventh or crown chakra, and discusses briefly the spiritual wisdom that comes to us in our maturity. In this section we can become more aware of our own behaviour patterns as we develop a greater ability for *self-reflection*.

The book can be read in its entirety and it can be read in sections. It embraces eastern and western philosophies and the beauty and intelligence contained within them. Each section is colour coded to the chakra that is the focus for that particular period, covering aspects of the practical and spiritual needs and development of both parent and child at this stage.

In your reading of this book I would urge the realisation that we all have the capacity to change the parts of us that no longer serve our purpose in life.

# The symbol of the lotus

*Until I visited Bali, I had never had the pleasure of seeing a real lotus flower, the leaves of the plant and its amazing seedpod. As I sat beside a beautiful pond covered with these peaceful blooms and the umbrella-like leaves held high above the water, I was infused with wonder and a feeling of serenity. I felt that in some way I had come home to a special part of myself. When I started to write this book I found where I could acquire a growing lotus, then purchased a large waterlily pot and placed it on my sun-drenched balcony. I filled it with rich mud and a deep layer of water into which I planted my baby lotus, and watched its life begin to unfold. I began to experience the 'lotus effect'.*

The lotus is a spectacular temperate-climate water plant. Its very large round leaves, shaped like those of the nasturtium and held high above water like umbrellas, shed water like mercury. The flowers also are very striking, being similar to broad-petalled waterlilies, with a curious watering-spout cone at their centre. This cone is the seedpod containing the fruit of the plant.

The lotus exhibits a special mud-repellent quality that has intrigued both mystics and scientists. It is now known that the lotus leaf is covered with an extremely dense layer of tiny pointed bumps. This gives the lotus its unique self-cleaning property, which scientists call the 'lotus effect'.

The lotus beautifies wetlands and ponds with its blooms, its leaves and its seedpods from summer until autumn. It hibernates in the cooler months. It is the only plant that fruits and flowers at the same time. As the buds and the blossoms and the seedpods of the lotus plant can be seen at the same time, it is regarded as an emblem of the past, the present and the future.

Seeds of the Indian lotus have been known to germinate hundreds of years after they are shed. An oriental sacred lotus seed collected from the sediment of a dry lake bottom near a small village in northeastern China has germinated after lying dormant for 1200 years. It is one of the oldest living seeds ever found.

In the Hindu tradition the traditional lotus of India has eight petals and, as there are eight major points of the compass in space, is the symbol of cosmic harmony. The lotus in Hinduism is seen as the self-born, immortal and spiritual nature of man. It represents the unfolding of all human possibilities, and of eternal regeneration, purity, beauty, longevity, health, fame and fortune – all qualities of desirable promise for a new child.

In Buddhism, the lotus symbolises faithfulness. The gold lotus of Taoism symbolises enlightenment, the *Tao* (the Way) or spiritual rebirth. The opening of the flower is believed to represent the development of the spiritual potential in humans. Chinese poets use the lotus flower to inspire people to continue striving through difficulties.

Ancient Egyptians revered the lotus flower as a symbol of purity and creative power. They decreed the lotus bud a symbol of the seed of manifestation.

Modern aromatherapy owes much to ancient Egypt, where the powerful healing properties of essential oils, derived from plants, were understood and used. Aromatherapy is a healing practice that uses essential oils in massage, baths or by inhalation to provide spiritual, emotional and physical relief and is now recognised by western health practitioners as a beneficial therapy. One of the attributes of aromatherapy is that it works on the mind and body simultaneously, making it a perfect, gentle medicine. The essential oil of the lotus is used for perfume and for relief of anxiety.

The lotus in eastern culture bears a similar symbolism to the rose in western christianity. The Rose of Sharon represents Christ and the christian church. This rose blooms in the harshness of arid desert conditions while the lotus rises and blooms in the muddy depths of water. Both the desert and the lake bed are challenging environments.

Symbolised by the life cycle of the lotus and budded in the shape of the cosmic egg, a human baby emerges from the waters of the womb, where he had his connection with its nourishing placenta through the umbilical cord. Reaching the surface, he is born to light and air and begins his physical unfolding. Just as a lotus blossoms, so does his consciousness, which rises from the instinctive mind (the muddy earth), grows through the intelligence of the manifest world (the waters) into absolute consciousness (the surface and the air) to blossom into divine wisdom (greeting the sun).

*As a symbol, the flower of the lotus can say more than words to enable us to understand our spiritual nature and the development of our consciousness in a modern world.*

# Energy centres of consciousness: the chakras

*I first learnt of the chakras when I took up the practice of yoga. I felt as if I had entered into a whole new realm of learning and self-discovery. This discovery has led me into an exploration of the senses; the nervous and endocrine systems; the spirituality of music; the energy of light and colour, and the wonderful world of myth and symbols. It also encouraged me to consider the value and beauty of eastern wisdom.*

*I have always been fascinated by the body's energy – the wonderful rush of love I experience when I hold a newborn child; the way that I contract when I am fearful or anxious; the excitement of sexual attraction; and the energy of wonderment that courses through me when I feel part of a sunset or swim with dolphins. What is happening to me when I have these different experiences, and where does the 'feeling' come from and ultimately go to? My orthodox learning has been founded in human bioscience and western science and in this learning I never found the answers to these questions.*

*It has been the yogic knowledge of Kundalini energy, the energy of the chakras, that has helped to open the door to my new understanding.*

All living creatures are made up of energy; our body cells vibrate with the subtle movements that are generated by a charge of electromagnetic energy, which enables each cell to carry out its individual function. We are energetic beings, and we are human because of the rate of vibration that resonates with our DNA, which contains the inherited genes found in the nucleus of each body cell. The exchange of nutrients and the taking up of oxygen is known as homeostasis, which maintains the body's balance and also helps to create our body energy. We express this in a positive way as warmth and vitality. If the energy is weak, we express ourselves in a more depressed or negative way. When this vibration of energy is no longer happening, then life is finished. The body gives up the spirit.

While all this vibration and energy happens in every living cell, there are certain areas of the body that have more concentrated energy centres. Each of these energy centres is known as a chakra, which is a Sanskrit word for wheel or circle. Shaped like a wheel, each chakra resembles a lotus flower with a specific number of petals. There are many energy centres or chakras in the human body, but in the Hindu tradition there are considered to be seven major ones, five of them situated in ascending order at the front of the spine. The sixth chakra is situated in the region of the 'third eye' (between our eyes) at the level of the brain stem (medulla oblongata) that joins the spinal cord to the brain. The seventh is situated in the region near the crown of the head, at the posterior fontanelle. This triangular-shaped membranous space at the junction of the parietal and occipital skull bones begins to ossify or become bone about six weeks after birth. This, in a baby, is often referred to as the fontanelle 'closing'.

Each of our chakras or energy centres corresponds to one of the ductless endocrine glands that are essential for hormone release into the blood stream. Hormones play an enormous part in our behaviour. For example, the adrenal gland, in response to a perceived threat, will release adrenalin into the blood system to act on the muscles required for fighting or for taking flight. The chakras are also associated with nerve plexuses, which are nerve networks situated on both the right and left sides of the spine and which enable interchange between the spinal nerves and the peripheral nervous system.

The chakras act as channels for the exchange of energies between the physical body and the non-physical etheric part of our aura, which interpenetrates our physical body. They are the centres that give out the personal energy created by our body, and they also act as channels to take in energies from the world around us. Have you ever felt someone else's energy before you have been aware of them through your other senses, such as seeing, hearing or smell? This is through your 'sixth sense', your intuition, which is a very powerful energetic sense that we all have the ability to tap into. When we love someone, or are 'in love', the energy that we feel deep within us is wonderful, yet we rarely wonder where that energy has been generated. This energy is our life energy, which keeps us living through all types of emotions. It gives us passion. We feel it in our body, we interpret it with our brain and we radiate it from within us. This energy is our 'aliveness'.

In eastern traditions, the chakras have been associated with the lotus blossom. A chakra is a spinning vortex or wheel of energy considered to be a spiritual and psychic centre of the body. When the centre is awakened, it begins to open and revolve like a wheel, its spokes resembling the petals of a lotus flower. From four petals at the base chakra to over a thousand at the crown, the number of petals of each energy centre expresses the centre's vibratory rate. Chakras are centres of *energy* in the etheric body of our aura which, like the energy of our thoughts or dreams, cannot be seen by ordinary sight nor measured by dissecting the physical body. However, people with clairvoyance are very aware of the chakras and the human aura, which is the energy that is within, and extends out from, our living physical body. This energy is known as the human energy field. When we are feeling the energy of another person, we are feeling their aura. Our sixth sense can 'feel' if that energy we are experiencing is 'good' or 'bad'.

The chakras are part of what might be regarded as our spiritual anatomy. Just as the physical body is laid out in an atlas of its physical anatomy visible to the naked eye, so too is our spiritual anatomy as viewed by individuals who have clairvoyance. The energy system of the living body is known as the subtle energy system and its energy, like electricity or magnetism, cannot be seen by the unknowing mind. The seven main chakras are a unified system – they rely on the energy of each other to function as a whole.

Once we learn of the chakras or energy centres and where they are situated, it becomes a little easier to understand each one. For example, the heart chakra, situated in the chest in the region of our heart, is the energy centre with which we are most in touch. When we are frightened or encounter a shock, our hand instinctively covers our heart in a protective movement. When we are 'in love' it is in the area of our heart that we feel so wonderful, as its energy centre expands and we want to open up to the whole world. We 'glow'.

As a system, the seven main energy centres or chakras express our patterns of behaviour and the progression of our development throughout our life. On the subtlest level, the chakras act as centres for facilitating the energy conversion between the physical body and the mind. As the centres awaken, they start to express the simple elements of the qualities of each chakra.

When we first learn to read, we start with the alphabet before we can progress to simple one-syllable words. From there we start to read simple sentences. It is a simple progression.

The understanding of the opening or blossoming of the chakras is a similar progression, we start with a simple knowledge.

It is the initial openings of the chakras that this book is concerned with, because this is the level at which a baby's energy centres are functioning. However, for your own self-awareness, the qualities of each energy centre or chakra are described so that you can learn to know yourself.

The following sections of this book are symbolised by the body's energy centres, the chakras, and their lotus petals, with each petal representing a month of life. In my view, the first 500-day period of a baby's development matches perfectly the specific behaviour accorded the first five energy centres and gives us a wonderful analogy of a child's behaviour.

*Within the pages of this book lies a new learning.*
*May our hearts and minds be open to what follows.*

# Conception to birth

During the pregnancy and birthing process, the mother goes on a spiritual journey of her own that in many ways mirrors the one her child will encounter once he is delivered into the world. The journey of this pregnancy is shared between mother and child and if the mother is able to understand and nurture this process her child will be born with a stronger connection to the spiritual core of himself and others.

Throughout the first three months of pregnancy, the womb and the baby are deep in the pelvis. It is during this time, while in the region of the mother's root chakra, that the embryo is developing the earthy parts of itself. During this period, the heart begins to beat, and gender is established. After nine weeks of development after fertilisation, when it has taken human form and all the life systems have been laid down, the embryo becomes a foetus.

At 12 weeks gestation, the baby begins to grow into the lower part of the abdomen in the region of the mother's second energy centre. At 24 weeks, the womb and its baby begins to grow into the mother's upper abdomen where her third energy centre is situated.

The first trimester, or three months of pregnancy, lays down the physical foundation of survival for the development of a new soul. This is the embryological period when the baby is most vulnerable to worldly environmental influences. It is in the second trimester, the period from three to six months, that pregnancy becomes movement and duality. This is the time of quickening, the first fluttering of a baby's movements felt within the womb. It is when a woman recognises that another life is growing within her. She speaks quite spontaneously to her baby, and also quite naturally and unconsciously massages him as she caresses her belly. As the pregnancy advances into the third trimester or last three months, the womb ascends into the upper abdomen in the region of the mother's solar plexus. This is the area of personal power and self-esteem. In this period a pregnant woman blossoms with confidence and self-expectation.

The birthing process starts with labour. This is when the expectant mother starts on a miraculous journey in a state of hope, excitement and nervous anticipation. This is the physical and emotional process of childbirth.

When labour begins, the baby begins his descent into the birth canal, through the region of the mother's first chakra. This is his first grounding experience as he passes through the birth canal. It is also the first grounding experience for the birthing mother who, in this second stage of labour, when the cervix is fully dilated, begins to come back to earth from the spiritual experience of the transition stage of the first stage of her labour.

The pain of giving birth can be exquisite and shocking. It brings a woman right down into her body, constantly and rhythmically. In the early stage of labour when the cervix dilates to 3cm and into the active stage of labour (4–7cm), a woman can endure the process if the labour is progressing well. She is fairly well grounded until she reaches the stage of transition. This time of transition, when her cervix dilates from 7cm to 10cm, is when she travels into a space within herself that she may never have been to before. It is a shock and it can be very confronting for her. This is the time when she may feel that she can no longer endure any more of the process. Socrates, when considering the nature of pain, described it not as one of the senses but as a passion of the soul. The labouring woman has a passion of her soul. It is the journey into her spiritual centre.

During the stage of transition, she cannot always tolerate being touched – it brings her too much into her body. This is when she is very emotionally vulnerable. In the time between the contractions, she goes deep into her soul space. Here, there is peace. If she is touched or spoken to she will react negatively. This can be quite a surprise for her support partner, who usually is the father of the baby and who is also emotionally involved in the birth. It is important that the father does not carry any hurt for this rejection, but instead can see it as a wonderful and positive move towards the moment of birth. In a normal labour, from the beginning of transition, the dilatation of the cervix and the descent of the baby progresses fairly rapidly.

It is like a turning point in the birth process. However, it is to be recognised that this is also a spiritual turning point for a woman, and she is going to spend the next 40 days, just as her baby will be, trying to come down from her spiritual centre to her earth, into her first energy centre, Muladhara.

In the first two to five days after the baby is born, the mother's breasts produce colostrum, a food that is easily digested, is nutritive, quenches thirst, is laxative in effect and contains immune bodies and vitamins. There is five times the amount of a substance called tryptophan in the colostrum than there is in breast milk. Tryptophan is an amino acid (protein), which, with the help of vitamin B6, serves as a precursor or aid for serotonin, a neurotransmitter or nerve messenger, which is important for sleep and for sensory perception. It could be the reduction from the high content of tryptophan in colostrum to the lower level in breast milk that causes the unsettled behaviour of a newborn when the 'milk comes in'.

When the colostrum changes to breast milk by about the fourth day, the breasts fill with the milk and sometimes become engorged with an increased blood supply. This can be very uncomfortable for the mother and difficult sometimes for the baby to attach properly to the breast to feed. Life can be a roller-coaster for a couple of days with plenty of emotions and tears. This is the beginning of grounding for both mother and baby. This experience, coupled with an initial discomfort of breastfeeding, frequent feeding and night waking, leads the mother into a state of weariness, when she longs to have time to sleep and return to her own inner peaceful and spiritual space.

Gradually over the next 100 days, the feeds shorten and are less frequent. By three months it all seems so easy and quick and leaves time for lots more worldly activity. Mother is back on earth.

This is when a mother's breasts seem to return to the state they were in just before the birth – they are softer and less swollen.

During the early weeks of the 'grounding' process, a woman can feel that her brain has turned to mush. Decisions are difficult to make, time runs away from her, the ability to organise anything beyond herself and her baby is a challenge. Nature did not intend a new mother to function with mental wizardry. The early weeks are a time for healing and nurturing herself physically and emotionally, and also for staying focused on her new baby and meeting his needs. Nature's intention is for a new mother and her baby to be nurtured and cared for by others, not the other way round.

When a new mother finds that she is able to function physically, mentally and emotionally, then the grounding process is almost complete. This process generally takes a little longer with the first baby; the body has memory and the healing is quicker with the second and subsequent babies. Even the process of making milk and feeding is quicker, and the body seems to be able to fend for itself earlier.

Nature is truly wonderful.

# SECTION I
# Sense of Self

# THE FIRST
# 100 DAYS

# MULADHARA
## *The Root Chakra*

# INTRODUCTION

When a baby is born into the world he is an extremely spiritual being who needs a lot of support to become part of the human race. He spends a great deal of his time in sleep where he maintains his spirituality. We are drawn to a sleeping baby; his energy is so amazing that we get in touch with a part of ourselves that uplifts us. I have seen 'tough' people melt into silent awe as they gaze upon a sleeping newborn miracle.

To survive as an earthling, a new baby needs to have food and touch and exercise. It is in these activities that babies become grounded. Some babies need more than others. They feed voraciously, they calm and stretch when they are gently massaged and they can exercise very strongly when they cry. Crying with long yelling breaths, feeding to take in earthly nourishment and being lovingly touched brings a baby into his body. When he has had enough grounding, he needs to be sleeping or resting in his spirit world where he finds peace and growth.

During the birthing period, or first 40 days, the new mother and her baby need to have a lot of time in their spirit world, the world of rest and daydream time. Rest and quietness and full support are essential for them to *gradually* become grounded. Our modern society demands so much of them both in this very special time. The newborn baby is over-handled and overstimulated. The newborn mother is stretched to a point of social and physical exhaustion. When this happens, neither mother nor baby is able to feed, sleep or function properly.

After the first 40 days, there is a change in how the mother feels about herself and her baby. Also, for the baby during the next two months, there is a gradual turn around as he begins to smile, has more awake time when he is more grounded, and his need to cry begins to lessen.

During the first three to four days, when he suckles at the breast, he takes small quantities of colostrum, which is 'spiritual' food. Colostrum is the food of transition, the first offering of the breast and the first food taken in by a newborn baby. Because it is taken in very small quantities, it acts like a cleansing fast.

The *fast* is a practice of many religions and cultures and is undertaken to enable humans to come close to God. It is a spiritual practice that allows contemplation and quietness for those who seek inner peace.

The baby loses a small amount of weight, mainly fluid, and also the meconium that has protected his gut while he was in the womb.

Even though it comes in small quantities, colostrum is rich in calories, disease-preventing antibodies and also substances that initiate sleep. That is why most babies are quite settled in this period. When there is a change from the colostrum to breast milk, which is a more grounding, earthly physical food, the baby can become very unsettled as he awakens from his spiritual state. This also happens for the mother, who can go through a very weepy stage as she begins to produce milk. It is in her weeping that a new mother becomes more grounded, as she begins to move away from her spiritual birth experience. The emotional roller-coaster ride between the spiritual and the physical for both a mother and her baby can be a very confusing and unsettling time. A lot of love and understanding and support are needed for the new mother.

*Parturition* is the separation of the baby from the mother's body, and it is not complete until six weeks have passed. There can be a type of grieving and some inner turmoil during this period, as it ushers in a more physical and earthly life of growth and development.

It is important that we understand that this is also the time of helping to bring a baby to earthly life, when the spiritual and physical are integrated into the whole being, and the emotional and mental natures of his *self* begin to develop. It is also the time of calling the parent to growth and wholeness through self-recognition and integration.

# The First Energy Centre

MULADHARA
'Root'

## *The Lotus of Four Petals*

The First 100 Days
Support and Survival

COLOUR: Red, which is full of power, energy and drive.
Wearing red can energise us and restore our confidence.

MUSIC: Drumming. A child, when feeling ungrounded and insecure, responds
well to rhythm.

SENSE: Smell. Mother, father, siblings and grandparents all have their own
unique smells that a baby can recognise and feel comforted by.

PHYSICAL SYSTEM: The kidneys, the blood and
the skeletal system.

ENDOCRINE SYSTEM: The adrenal gland.

ANIMAL TOTEM: Elephant; one of the most spiritual yet grounded of all God's
creatures. The elephant has the strength of sacred wisdom.

# MULADHARA – GROUNDING

The first 100 days of a baby's life can be likened to the first chakra, the energy centre located in the area of the body that is near the front of the coccyx at the base of the spine. This energy centre is concerned with our most basic consciousness – survival. It is our centre of belonging, of being part of a family, a social group, humanity, our world and the cosmos. It is also our centre of inner stillness.

These first 100 days are the baptism or initiation into a life of growth. It is the foundation of things to come. The sense associated with this chakra is smell, and in the first 100 days this is the most developed of the senses.

The first energy centre, called the root chakra, is represented by four petals, which I view as the first four months of life. The first 100 days, like the first chakra, relate to our grand human potential, our primitive energy and our basic survival needs. It is survival through animal instinct. The primitive reflexes observed in a new baby are present to help ensure this survival. The stepping reflex, observed when a newborn, held upright, lifts one foot after the other in a walking movement, ensures that the baby can use his feet to push his way from the birth canal to the mother's breast. The rooting reflex, when a baby will turn his head to something touching his cheek, ensures that he can find the nipple; the sucking reflex ensures that he can take in the nourishment that he needs. The startle reflex, which happens when a baby is startled by a sudden noise or movement, represents his need for safety. His limbs extend before flexing to cling at anything within reach, just as our primitive ancestor would cling to his mother's fur or the branch of a tree.

Most of these reflexes are regarded as primitive. They are controlled by the primitive areas of the brain situated in the brain stem and areas of the limbic system. As connections to the higher centres of the brain develop over the first three or four months after birth, the baby's movements become smoother and more coordinated.

At the end of his first 100 days, as the baby becomes grounded, these reflexes are no longer needed, so they gradually disappear as the baby begins to master some survival skills to maintain his connection to body and earth.

You will know when your baby is becoming more grounded because he will begin to 'weight-bear'. His legs will straighten, and he will have pleasure in almost standing when you hold him in your lap. Don't force a baby's 'weight-bearing', he will do it in his own time. A lot of babies achieve it at three months of age. Some babies take a lot longer. It depends on their ability and readiness to be earthed.

The root chakra draws energy from the magnetic centre of the earth, up through our feet and legs, to give grounding energy to the blood and tissue cells of our body. This energy keeps us grounded in our material worldly existence. What joy there is to stand or sit on a large rock that has been kissed by the sun. The energy generated by the rock's atomic structure radiates comfort and brings our attention back to mother earth and her natural wonders. In the same way, a baby loves to have his feet gently massaged by the warm hands of someone who is well grounded as this helps to bring him more fully into his physical earthly body.

For a mother, the ability to nurture her baby depends on her ability to nurture herself, and if she has a strong and balanced root energy centre, then the greater possibility she has of a positive and normal birth experience. If she brings to her own birthing experience the negative attitudes and myths of her family or her cultural upbringing, then she may find the whole experience a difficult one. This is the result of an unbalanced root chakra and her journey will require a look at how she can bring more balance to it. It is then that a new mother's earthing experience can be more fulfilling.

This chakra is where we form the boundaries in our life. It is where we defend our life, formulate our attitudes, adopt family and cultural attitudes, and take on physical challenges.

Providing a baby with some physical boundaries can help him to be secure and grounded. Up until the time of birth, the baby's physical environment has been in a foetal position in a snug womb. Providing him with the physical feeling of this snugness by swaddling him can really help him to feel safe. When he is having his bath, a warm wet face cloth on his chest is another way. By the end of his first 100 days, when he is more grounded, he doesn't need these security methods as often as his early days. He becomes more open to change.

# THE BEHAVIOUR
# OF A NEWBORN CHILD
## DOWN-TO-EARTH CONSCIOUSNESS

This first or base chakra is the energetic core of a baby's security and survival instincts. It enables him to stay deeply connected to himself and to his environment. It is his instinctive mind and it is the foundation in his ultimate quest for self-knowledge. If his needs are met in this period then he grows up confidently, knowing that all his requirements for survival, food, drink, warmth and safety are available. Eventually, in adulthood, this will also involve his attitudes to money and to material necessities.

Biologically, this time for a baby is the period when his development can be considered to be primitive. It is the development that comes at the beginning of life, as a foundation for the development of higher levels of behaviour.

Emotionally, it is the time for 'grounding', or for consciousness to come fully into the body, and for developing a beginning sense of his own personal self and personal safety. It is also a centre of belonging – his inner sense is of being part of another, particularly his mother. It is also the centre of 'being' and of 'having enough' for a happy and meaningful existence: health, love and security.

Physically, it marks rapid growth, particularly in the connections between the cells of the brain. In the beginning, all the brain cells, numbered in the billions, are present, but because the connections between them have not grown and developed the insulation in a process known as myelination (which enables messages to pass quickly between the cells), the baby's movements are uncoordinated and his vision limited. His senses of smell, taste and hearing are fairly well refined because these centres of the brain are situated in the brain stem, the part of the brain which is considered to be 'primitive' and which is fairly well organised at birth.

Brain cell connections take longer to develop in premature babies. Consequently, it takes a little longer for these babies to reach their milestones in physical and emotional development. They also stay a little longer in their spirit world, and their fontanelles or 'soft spots' at the top of their heads are quite open and the skull sutures are wider and softer.

When observing a new baby's behaviour, it is important to take into consideration whether he was born earlier or later than the due birth date. If born earlier, then he may take a little longer to grow into his development stages. If later, then he may grow into these stages earlier.

## TIRED SIGNS

In the first 100 days a baby needs to be settled and will need a lot of sleep, as it is during the sleeping hours that he will gain the energy he needs to connect to his new life. Sleep also gives him respite from the huge changes which are taking place around him. However, for many new parents tired signs can often be confused with hunger because there is a lot of mouth action and often a bit of noise.

Tired signs are confused with what we think is pain or 'colic' because a baby will often draw his legs up in an effort to get himself into the foetal position and back into the womb, or he may go rigid like a banana because he is so overtired. So, here are some clues to basic tired signs in a new baby.

**Frowning:** One minute, a baby can appear content, then loses eye contact with you and looks away. There may be a definite frown over the forehead and eyes.

**Clenched fists:** When a baby's hands are no longer open and relaxed but are tightly closed it is because he is tense with tiredness.

**Hand-to-mouth action:** This is a fairly haphazard action and he can end up scratching his cheek or eyes, when what he is attempting to do is suck on a finger or thumb in order to comfort himself.

**Jerky movements:** This is especially noticeable with his arm movements.

**Yawning:** When a yawn happens, it is a sign of a release in a baby's system, like a sigh. After the first month, when a baby is requiring a little less sleep, then a yawn is a very good sign. This is because the body becomes tense as he tires, the breathing becomes shallow and the oxygen intake is low, so the body responds by yawning to boost the oxygen levels. It is also thought that yawning releases a lubricating substance, surfactant, into the less used areas of the lungs that do not fully inflate when breathing is shallow. Shallow breathing is the result of a tight diaphragm, tense muscles, shoulders held high and an anxious tummy.

If a baby's tired signs are ignored or if a distraction is used to try and stop them, then it becomes much more difficult to settle the baby. The more he is handled, the louder and more desperate he becomes. Red in the face, body unrelaxed and stiff, he ends up being rocked frantically, having a toy jangled in his face, or being passed from one person to the next with a hope that he will calm. He probably won't like it.

*A baby needs help to settle and sleep as soon as he gives his tired sign.*

## SLEEPING

Western cultures demand a lot of new babies and their parents, without understanding that for a new baby 'going to sleep' without any help is a skill he needs to learn. It takes time and readiness, not only for the baby but also for the parent. It is also a 'process', and the parents are the only ones to decide when and if they and their baby are ready for it. When a baby is overstimulated, over-handled and consequently overtired, it takes him a lot longer to go to sleep and he will do a lot of crying, because that is the only way that he can discharge his stress. This discharge of stress or body tension is necessary before the body can relax and enter a state of sleep.

During the birthing period or the first 40 days following delivery, a baby needs six to eight feeds in a 24-hour period. This has a lot to do with the size of his stomach. At birth, the stomach is the size of a large marble and, over the next few weeks this capacity increases, until at one month of age his stomach is the size of a squash ball. It also has a lot to do with his emotional and spiritual needs.

A new baby needs to have these feeding opportunities in order to have frequent opportunities for grounding himself. Grounding happens with taking in milk, being gently touched by family and with the exercise that comes with crying. When he has had enough earthing, he will give us his tired sign so that he can return to his dreamy 'spirit' world of sleep.

## How much sleep does a baby need?

On average, a newborn baby will sleep about 16½ hours in a 24-hour day. This is broken into four day sleeps and longer sleeps over an eight and a half-hour period at night.

*If a baby is having six to eight feeds in the 24 hours, and the feeding process takes about an hour with nappy change, giving the feed, burping, wrapping and back to bed, it can be seen that six to seven hours have gone in 'baby activity'. This is about as much 'up' time that a baby can manage for the first few weeks.*

By four weeks of age, the baby will sleep an average, 15½ hours in the 24-hour day, with three longer day-sleep periods and longer sleeps over a nine-hour period at night.

By now the feed times will be reducing a little, you will have more confidence in bathing, changing and general 'doing' for the baby, and baby will become more sociable – he may even be smiling occasionally. Now you can enjoy a little more 'up' time with him, even though he still does not need playtime or entertainment.

At three months of age the baby will sleep an average of 15 hours in 24, with three shorter day sleeps and a longer night sleep period of seven to ten hours. Now we're talking good times! The baby might even be sleeping through from the last feed in the evening, say at 9 or 10pm, to the early morning feed at 5 or 6 am. He will be content to have playtime and there will even be lovely times of 'talking' together.

Some babies become daytime cat-nappers, but if a baby is sleeping well at night then this is not a concern. Sleep engenders sleep, and when a baby does not sleep well at night it may be an indication that he is not having enough sleep (or food) *for him as an individual* during the daytime.

If a baby is sleeping well at night, then it is a sign that he is having enough sleep during the daytime.

> *One definition of sleep is 'dormancy' or 'inactivity'. Sometimes a 'quietly sleeping baby' can in fact be resting in his bed quite peacefully with his eyes wide open. This quiet time that he is having with himself can also be regarded as his sleep time. Some babies have quite a lot of 'quiet' time, and when they have had enough, they will call out for you.*

## A new baby's sleep pattern

If a baby is put to bed while still awake, he will learn to put himself to sleep. This is fairly difficult to do in the beginning because he hasn't yet learnt the skill of drifting off to sleep on his own. Most times he needs some sort of aid or comfort to help him get to sleep, such as patting, rocking, the breast, the bottle, the pram, the car, the dummy, holding, sleeping in your bed with you, etc. The trouble with all of this is that baby will generally stay asleep for about 20 to 30 minutes and then the whole process has to be repeated. This is very exhausting for you, particularly if you have stairs to climb or you are trying to get some sleep yourself. It is also exhausting for your baby because he has to keep calling out to you to come and help him to get back to sleep. Understanding his sleep pattern will help you to understand why he does this.

Our sleeping state consists of many cycles of two different types of sleep, light sleep and REM (rapid eye movement) or deep sleep. A newborn baby has a sleep cycle that lasts for about 50 minutes during which time he spends half of his sleep time in light sleep and the other half in deep sleep. There will be two to three sleep cycles while he is asleep as the following illustration shows:

## Newborn Sleep Pattern

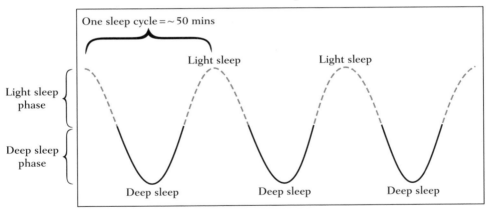

Now let's look at what happens when a baby has an aid to go to sleep and why he will only stay asleep for a short time. I use the example of the breast as an aid. When the baby goes to the breast, his eyes are open and he feeds heartily. Gradually, his eyes will close, and he will have a little munch time, then a rest, then another munch time, then a rest, etc. When he is doing this he is in light sleep until he eventually passes into deep sleep and slips away from the breast. So we put him into bed, and 20 to 30 minutes later he is awake and calling out to us. This is because he has reached the next light phase of the sleep cycle. If the aid that helped him to go to sleep in the beginning is no longer there (in this case, the breast), he will wake himself up looking for it so that he she can go into deep sleep again.

# Sleep development

A newborn baby has a biological 'hour' or time cycle of about 50 minutes, whereas in adulthood the biological 'hour' or time cycle is about 90 minutes. After 90 minutes, the adult brain loses its full concentration and needs to be relieved and refreshed. This is essential when driving a car on long journeys. It is also the maximum time that we can concentrate when learning in the classroom. So for a new baby, it is easier to understand he is ready for sleep after his biological 'hour' or time cycle of 50 to 60 minutes of 'up' time.

Rapid eye movement (REM) sleep accounts for 50 per cent of a new baby's sleep cycle. This gradually decreases over the next three months when, at the end of this 100-day period, REM sleep accounts for 40 per cent of the sleep cycle. It is believed that the active REM sleep stimulates the brain and during this activity the brain continues to develop the connections between the neurones or brain cells.

The non-REM or inactive sleep stage of sleep is when the body refreshes and rejuvenates itself.

When a term baby is newly born, his sleeping pattern starts in the stage of light active or rapid eye movement (REM) sleep, which is why he finds 'going to sleep and staying asleep' difficult. This gradually changes over the first 100 days, when at about three to four months of age he will begin his sleep cycle in the deeper sleep stage, a pattern he will continue to develop into adolescence.

Helping a baby to learn to put himself to sleep in this period may provide a good foundation for him to become a 'good sleeper' in the future.

# Sleeping position

It is currently believed that sleeping on the back is the preferred option for a new baby. This can be a very difficult position for a newborn baby to settle in to when he is fresh from the foetal position in the womb. If you are positioning the baby on his back to sleep, then it is advisable to alternate his head position from side to side and to maintain that position by slightly turning his pelvis (hips) to face the same direction. This will help to prevent him from developing a preference of head direction and a consequent development of tight muscles in his neck and a slightly out-of-shape head. As a baby grows stronger he will move his head from side to side, but it is good to develop an awareness of his neck flexibility through alternating his head position when he goes to bed.

# Noises in the night

Babies are very noisy creatures and not only when they are awake. You have probably discovered that your baby is very noisy when sleeping, particularly if, sleeping close to you. Don't be alarmed. Try to sleep through all the grunts, farts, squirms and dreams. An alternative is to move him into his own space if the noises are disturbing your sleep.

# Sleeping environment

Many first new babies spend a lot of time in a room where the window coverings are closed and there is no background noise. If he is having the occasional unsettled day, then this may be a good idea, but to have this situation every day does not help him to grow up to be a flexible little person in a happening, noisy world. It also means that the family will have to stay home to provide this type of environment all the time. This does not seem like much fun.

A baby hears sounds while in the womb, so household noise is familiar and it may be comforting to have you close by. Baby generally likes and needs to be part of the rhythm of life.

Second and subsequent babies grow up with all sorts of sibling bangs and crashes going on around them and seem to be able to sleep through it.

Most babies learn to sleep through car and traffic noise and in the daylight while they are on an outing. If it is possible for you to let your baby have day sleeps in a light environment with background family noise, then it will serve you both in the long run. Hearing laughter is good for the soul, even when we are sleeping. Laughter elevates the spirit and has been proven to nurture our immune system and promote healthy growth.

Light is an element essential for our healthy growth and development. Apart from 90 per cent of coloured light reaching the organs of the body through the eyes, information about light and colour also enters the body through the skin. It is known that light enters the unborn child while in the womb.

Light is especially essential for the pineal and pituitary glands, situated deep in the brain. These endocrine glands produce hormones that stimulate other glands throughout the body, thereby affecting body metabolism.

Experiments have demonstrated that visually impaired people are affected by colour in the same way as the sighted. Some are sensitive enough to identify a colour with great accuracy by feeling the density of the air around it. For example, the air around red is denser than the air surrounding blue.

People who are deprived of sufficient daylight can be prone to a type of depression known as SAD or 'seasonal affective disorder'. This can happen because they spend a lot of their time indoors in artificial light, or they may live in a latitude where the sun is absent for a prolonged period of the year. Conversely, excessive exposure to light can accelerate development and hasten the ageing process. It is therefore probably a good idea for a baby to grow up with the *natural* rhythm of the day and to learn to sleep in an environment of daylight (short sleeps) and night time (long sleep).

## FEEDING

The food for new babies in the first four to six months is either breast milk or baby formula milk. Quantities vary from baby to baby, with some babies needing large amounts and some babies thriving on less than the recommended guidelines. If a baby is gaining weight of about 150 grams a week and having at least six good wet/poo nappies each day, then he is feeding well. Some babies may only gain 100 grams one week and 200 grams the next, but they average out at 150 grams. Another baby may gain as much as 300 grams a week! Look at how content a baby is and how he is developing. Often babies follow the same growth patterns of their parents and of their parent's siblings when they were babies, so try to find out your family growth history.

By about two weeks of age a baby needs to be offered both breasts at each feed. This does not mean that he will drink from the second breast each time, but he needs to have the opportunity to feed as much as he needs. The feed time will still be 30 to 40 minutes with 25 to 30 minutes at the first breast and five to ten minutes at the second. These feed times will reduce over the next six to eight weeks as the breast and the baby become more efficient. If there is a concern about how much milk a baby is receiving from the breast, always look at what is coming out of him. It is all a matter of fluid balance: what goes in (*fluid or 'input'*) comes out (*wee/poo or output*).

# SETTLING

Even though knowing that crying is a natural event for a new baby, having a crying baby can still be a very stressful time for new parents. This is because a baby's cry is so compelling that we have the urge to stop the crying and we can't always achieve it.

A new baby cries on average two to three hours in a 24-hour period. A new baby doesn't cry in the same way that we as adults cry. A baby yells. This involves opening the mouth wide and, in so doing, moving the bones of the skull, the spine and the pelvis as well as the jaw. This is how he adjusts the alignment of the bony parts of his body following the birth delivery. Some babies need more adjusting than others. It all depends on the mechanics of their birth or delivery and the position that they adopted in the womb.

## The positives of crying

While observing a crying baby, some very good physical activity can be seen. Consider that crying, for a new baby, is not an emotional experience at this age, it is a physical one. Physical activity is grounding activity.

Crying is the only opportunity that a new baby has to fully expand his lungs so that they can develop and become healthy. If you observe a baby when he is deeply asleep, it is almost impossible to see him breathing, because it is so shallow. The body is resting, there is no exercise and his full lung capacity is not being used.

Crying is also the only way that a new baby can unwind and discharge the excess energy and excitement that has built up during his 'awake' period. Older infants, children and adults have an opportunity to blow off this built- up energy with talking and with physical exercise such as crawling, walking and running around. If you hold your hand close to your mouth as you exhale strongly you can feel the warmth. This is spent energy that comes with your breath.

# How much crying is there?

From about two to nine weeks of age after a full-term pregnancy, a baby will have one unsettled period in a day and one unsettled day in a week. This seven-week period can be a tiring time for you and baby. The unsettled period can extend between two feeds, when the baby will be wakeful and/or crying and may only sleep fitfully. Often this period is in the evening when you are tired, the milk supply may be running a little low and you are also trying to prepare and eat your own meal. *It may make it easier to tolerate if you can imagine that there are only about 49 of these unsettled periods (seven days by seven weeks).*

The unsettled day is often on a Sunday or Monday, because a baby is handled a lot at weekends – in and out of the car capsule, the pram, bed, out visiting, having visitors, etc (he becomes a 'pass-the-parcel' baby).

*Imagine that there will be about seven unsettled days.*

A baby may start to cry about 20 to 30 minutes after the end of a feed because he is tired. There are scientific theories that suggest that when food reaches upper sections of our gut, a message is relayed to the brain that says 'sleep'. This probably explains why we feel so sleepy after eating a heavy meal, such as Christmas dinner.

The amount of time that a new-term baby spends crying, and the intensity of the crying, generally peaks at about six weeks after birth. From then on a baby will spend less time crying and more time awake during the daytime as he becomes a more social little person and begins to smile and vocalise in response to you.

A baby's crying is most desperate when he is overtired. When a baby cries with great intensity, his little face will become very red and sweaty and he will reach a stage of almost holding his breath. This is quite distressing for anyone who can hear him, but often if a baby is able to move through this frenzy, he will fall asleep and sleep very well. This is because when a baby cries like this, he hyperventilates and breathes out too much carbon dioxide. The brief holding of breath stops this process so that the body then feels more comfortable, the baby relaxes and he is then able to put himself to sleep.

# TYPES OF CRYING

### HURTING CRY

*If you have heard a baby cry when he had his heel pricked for his new-born screening test, you would have heard him scream with a high-pitched cry. That is his cry of pain.*
*The cry of pain has a sudden onset and a high intensity.*

### HUNGER CRY

*This is the cry that comes around two to four hours after the beginning of his last feed. It is a medium-pitched and medium-intensity cry. It generally starts with whimpering that is interspersed with short quiet periods.*

### TIRED CRY

*This cry starts with grizzling or grunting and can develop into a deep growl. It is quite gutteral and may accompany a lot of hand-to-mouth action and stiffening or arching of the body.*

### 'SOMETHING WRONG' CRY

*This can be a concern and even difficult to define. If you feel intuitively that there is something wrong, and tiredness or hunger is ruled out, then seek medical advice as soon as possible. If you are not hearing an answer that you feel comfortable with, then seek out a second opinion.*

## ALWAYS TRUST YOUR INTUITION

### WET NAPPY CRY

*Generally, a new baby is only uncomfortable with a wet/poo nappy if he is tired. Babies at this age manage to sleep for long periods with very full nappies, and not complain. When he wakes he would rather feed than have his nappy changed first.*

# How long can you let a baby cry?

You may let a baby cry for as long as you can cope with it. In the early days this may only be for a very short time, but as time passes it becomes easier as confidence builds and you become more familiar with the little person in your care. The time to work on this confidence building is in the morning. Somehow it is easier to cope with a crying baby when the sun is up, you are refreshed from sleep and there are plenty of chores to be done. Instead of taking too much notice of the clock, make a pact with the baby when you put him to bed that you will return to him *if he needs you* after you have washed your hair, or had your shower, or washed the dishes, or hung the washing to dry, or finished one of the other millions of things that need to be done.

The emphasis on *if he needs you* is important, because *listening* to him crying is different from *hearing* him cry. When responding to a baby, pause to listen and determine whether he is in control. Is his cry winding down, Is he completely 'losing it'? Is he just grizzling? Pause to listen and learn. *Crying* is his experience. *Hearing his crying* is ours.

# Listen before responding

When you pause to listen to a baby's crying, take a very deep breath and let it out very slowly so that your shoulders relax, your tummy unwinds and your buttock muscles drop. *Then* make your decision whether to respond or not. If you make a decision to respond, here are some suggestions:

Change his position in bed without lifting him from it. If you have him on his side, change sides. If he is on his back, adjust his head and pelvis position. (When we are sleeping or trying to go to sleep, we adjust our position until we feel comfortable. In other words, we toss and turn during sleep.)

Use the dummy.

If he is lying on his side, place your hands on his body (shoulder and hip) and gently 'rock' him a few times.

Gently stroke his forehead with your finger with downward movements that start at the hairline and continue down towards the tip of the nose. This not only calms your child, it encourages his eyes to close.

Swaddle or wrap him securely.

# The dummy

Every healthy term baby is born with a suck reflex, along with about 30 other primitive reflexes, such as the startle reflex, the step reflex and the rooting reflex. These reflexes start to disappear at about the time that the unsettled two to nine week period disappears, and most babies do not have them after 12 to 14 weeks of age. Satisfying the suck reflex and the startle reflex is one way to help a newborn baby to settle.

The dummy is a wonderful comfort for a baby who has a very strong suck reflex and avoids the use of the breast or bottle to satisfy his need to suck and suck and suck. When first offered the dummy, a baby may need some help to accept it. A simple cherry-shaped dummy usually does the trick. If it is introduced just behind the top gum and directed towards the roof of the mouth, he will not gag and reject it. Allow him to suck/draw it into his mouth.

If he is very unsettled, calm him first of all with your clean finger in the same way. When he has calmed, withdraw your finger and insert the dummy.

While a dummy is an excellent comfort in the first 100 days, it is a good idea for baby to be weaned from the dummy by about the age of four months.

The reason for this is that at about seven to eight months of age, it is quite normal for a baby to wake three or four times in a night, talk to the fairies and then put himself back to sleep. If a baby needs a dummy to help him back to sleep and is unable to find it in the night, guess who has to. *It will be you.* And you will need to do it three or four times every night! *This often results in very tired, resentful and cranky parents and very tired and cranky babies.*

# Socks

A baby, like most adults and children, is unable to sleep soundly if he has cold feet. So if he is not sleeping as soundly as you would like, it is probably because he needs a pair of socks on his feet before being dressed in his baby suit.

# Swaddling

A baby spends nine months in the womb – a warm and cosy environment, rocked by the mother's movements and lulled by the rhythm of her heartbeat.

Towards the end of pregnancy, life in the womb begins to be a bit of a squash, so most babies wrap themselves in a ball, with their chin on their chest, their arms crossed in front of them and their knees and legs tucked up towards their tummy. This is known as the foetal position. When a newborn baby is not in this position, he can feel very uncomfortable and not nurtured, so when swaddling a baby to settle, try to create the foetal position for him. This is one method of swaddling:

Use a soft, light wrap, or bassinette sheet (in summer, a muslin wrap is ideal). If rectangular in shape, fold over a good 20cm of one long side. If the wrap is squarer in shape, fold over a generous corner to reach towards the centre of the wrap.

Place the base of the baby's head on the fold line and tuck one of his arms well into the fold. Then tuck that end of the fold securely around his waist so that his arm is folded across his chest. Repeat this with his other arm.

Now lift him up and hold his 'head up' against your chest and encourage his head to fold towards his chest, at the same time tucking his folded legs towards his tummy. *Breathe.*

Place the baby in his bed, preferably with his legs propped in the foetal position either against the end of his crib or cot, or bolstered with a folded towel. This prevents his legs from straightening and his head from extending back, exposing his vulnerable heart chakra.

This method of swaddling allows a baby some movement of his arms without being disturbed by the startle (Moro) reflex, as well as freedom of his chest. If a baby can move his arms, then it encourages his breathing.

Sometimes a baby appears to struggle against his wrap, probably because he is very, very tired. If he is a baby who can settle with his hands free and not scratch or damage himself, then swaddle him as he likes it.

# The bath

Another luxury of the womb is the relaxing warm fluid that baby bathes in. If you have tried to settle baby without success, then a warm bath may help to calm him, particularly if he has recently been fed. A baby will enjoy a bath a lot more if he has food in his tummy.

When he is undressed for the bath, place him on his tummy and, with warm hands, gently massage his feet, then move up his body, massaging with downward strokes. This can be very pleasurable for a baby, particularly if he is on his tummy and his chest and heart chakra are protected by the surface on which he is lying. This position also allows for 'tummy time' when he can lift his head and strengthen the muscles at the back of his neck.

If the baby feels vulnerable and anxious in the bath, place a warm wet face cloth across his chest and heart. When he is being dressed, a clean dry cloth on his chest will also keep him feeling safe and he may cling to it while you complete the dressing process. The heart chakra is the chakra with which we are most in touch, and the one that we most want to protect. Whenever we feel insecure or upset, our hand intuitively covers our heart in a protective movement. *A new baby always tries to protect his heart chakra.*

# The very, *very* unsettled baby

Some healthy babies seem to be incredibly unsettled in their first 100 days. For no obvious reason, they seem to cry louder and for longer than other babies do. Their families need a lot of relief, support and nurturing from relatives, friends, neighbours and health professionals to help them through these early months. If the crying continues, a complete medical check-up of baby with your family doctor or paediatrician is necessary. Complementary therapies, such as cranio-sacral therapy or naturopathy, with accredited practitioners can often help.

Take heart, for these little babies usually develop into the most delightful and happy people.

# THE EARTHING OF
# A NEW PARENT

The birthing process begins with the birth of a baby and it does not end until 40 days later. This has been forgotten in many western cultures. Some cultures, such as Greek or Asian, still acknowledge these six weeks as a very special time, not only for the newborn baby but also for the woman who has just given birth. For women of the Victorian era it was known as the 'lying in' period, when a newly delivered woman remained in her home to rest and heal, to be nurtured by the women of her family or community. In our modern times, a woman is allowed only a matter of hours of resting before visitors arrive to view the newborn baby and mother. When they depart, they often leave behind an exhausted, weeping mother and baby, a confused father and sometimes fractured tensions between them.

## What is happening to us as a couple?

When a baby comes into a couple's life, it is a miracle. With this miracle come many life adjustments to be realised. Family social life is turned upside down, and there can be an almost overwhelming feeling of new responsibility and commitment with a recognition that it will be like this for a long span of time. There is exhaustion. There is a 24-hour daily commitment of nurturing, learning, coping and growing. There is broken sleep and sometimes it may feel like there is no sleep at all.

This is a time for gentle healing and acceptance, especially for yourself and each other.

There is crying – let it happen. How rich we are, as humans, to have tears, which wash and release us. In the 40 days, the body lets go. It leaks. The womb releases the baby, the afterbirth and its juices. The breasts let go and 'leak'. And the tears continue to flow. Gradually this letting go lessens and completes by five to six weeks after the birth and new strength comes.

All of this is part of the miracle. It is the parent's grounding process.

*This miracle is all part of a spiritual experience
when we reach into the places in our soul that we may not
have travelled before.*

Occasionally, some very uncomfortable feelings rise up in newborn parents. When everything possible has been done to settle a baby, and the crying continues, then often a parent can have feelings of resentment, or feelings of failure or the feeling that she is 'losing it'. When this happens, acknowledge those feelings and remove yourself from the baby. Reach out to someone and let that person know how you are feeling. If there is nobody there for you at a time of extreme feeling within you, place baby in bed where he is quite safe and walk outside your home. Walk to the letterbox, to the front gate or even to the corner of the street. Your baby is safe in bed. Reach out to anyone, even someone you don't know, and tell that person how you are feeling. In talking about our feelings we often discharge the energy that comes with them and can often dissolve a lot of its intensity. Writing our feelings down on paper helps discharge this energy as well. Just let the pen flow, the grammar and spelling do not need to be perfect. Nor do the words need to make sense. Just write. The act of writing or verbalising seems to be able to discharge the negativity around the feelings.

A baby in our life is a miracle.

*It is NOT OK to allow our anger and frustration to harm a baby.*

# PARENTING WITH SECURITY, ENERGY AND SUSTAINABILITY

Through human evolution, we possess all the qualities we need for our survival. The rush of adrenalin released in times of stress is the gift of our endocrine system. It comes from the cortex of the adrenal glands that sit just on top of our kidneys, and through this hormone we are able to fight or take flight. The power of the mind enables us to be grounded, to plant our feet firmly on the earth. When we feel strong we are better able to deal with the challenges that life gives us. Even our thoughts can control our stress levels.

When we are positively grounded, we become the mothers or nurturers of the earth, whether we are male or female. Our environment is our garden, where our children, like plants, are encouraged to grow straight and tall, to hold hope and confidence in their endeavours and have complete faith in the survival of the individual and in the healing of scars. We feel strong in our ability to nurture all living things

If we are not properly grounded we become a victim – a person unable to stand on their own two feet, a person who believes that the universe is conspiring against them. Victims move through life dependent on others, expecting the world to fix their problems. Victims simply do not cope with the challenges of life.

We all face stress in our life from time to time, so if we can learn to deal with stress or change without giving up and becoming a victim of circumstance, then we find our inner resourcefulness. This can build our self-confidence so that the next time we meet a challenge in life, we know we have the strength to grow through it.

Parenting is one of the greatest challenges of life. It involves change and it demands flexibility. It also demands absolute commitment, and once we make the decision to mother and nurture life then there is no turning back or sidestepping the responsibility that we have chosen. Realising this commitment; not only socially but also environmentally and economically, demands balancing the fulfilment of physical needs with the resources available. This requires our inner strength, our outer abilities and the wisdom that we gain as we move through life.

External circumstances play an enormous part in how we become grounded. Often, if a challenge is almost overwhelming, we revert to our basic instincts for our survival. There is a need to return to our roots, our family or the community that we were born to. We yearn for the safety of the familiar. What is necessary in these times of need is a connection with what is real. If we can maintain a grip on reality then we can handle change.

However comforting this may be, if we become overly attached to the familiar we retard our personal growth. This is why, as parents, flexibility is essential. It requires acceptance of other points of view, of different ways of doing things, and a resolve to create universal change for the better. There are children in the world growing up in an environment of bombs and hatred. These children are growing up thinking that violence is the normal way of living. If they can be nurtured and taught to be flexible; to consider different ways of living and of doing things, then they can have hope and confidence of change. Parenting in a rapidly changing world requires flexibility and it behoves us to bring this to whomever and whatever we choose to nurture. To be flexible requires great love.

*If you can dream –*
*and not make dreams your master,*
*If you can think – and not make thoughts your aim,*
*If you can meet with Triumph and Disaster*
*And treat those two impostors just the same …*
*Yours is the earth and everything that's in it,*
*And which is more, you'll be a Man, my son!*

RUDYARD KIPLING

# THE SECOND
## 100 DAYS

# SVADISTHANA

## *The Sacral Chakra*

# INTRODUCTION

The second 100 days of a baby's life covers the period from 14 weeks or three and a half months through to 28 weeks or about seven months. This is a wonderfully exciting and responsive time for a baby. This is when physical exploration begins. New eating experiences happen, she begins to move distances by rolling and by pushing with her feet, and she responds with such obvious pleasure to familiar surroundings, situations and people.

The first three and a half months after the birth of a baby is a time for parent and child to start getting to know each other, for learning the different tired signs, types of crying, how and when to feed and some settling techniques. It is also a time for parents to learn a lot about themselves, their partner, parents and friends, as you deal with the reality of the new baby in your life, feeling emotions you may not have experienced before.

During the second 100 days of life, a baby begins to individuate. Individuation is the process of forming an individual existence separate from another person. She is becoming her *own* identity, developing a sense of self.

During this period a baby's colour vision further develops. Her eyes become so big and clear and seductive. Her hands start reaching out to grab.

The noise can be amazing – laughing, babbling and shrieking, the sound of which can startle even the baby herself.

This is when a baby may start sleeping through the night, allowing parents more rest and the opportunity of regaining some of their lost social lives. A mother's body regains pre-pregnancy state and she tends to gain more confidence, both in herself and her ability to deal with her new child. There is less anxiety about 'getting it right'.

This is a time for resting, rejuvenating and truly experiencing the joys that a new baby brings. It is a truly delightful period, and one that can be enjoyed before this little person *really* gets on the move.

Happiness!

# The Second Energy Centre

SVADISTHANA

'Sweetness'

## *The Lotus of Six Petals*

The Second 100 Days

The Seat Of Life – My Own Abode – Intimacy

COLOUR Orange, traditionally the colour of stimulation, strengthens the etheric body in the same way that the colour red stimulates the physical body.

SENSE Taste: during this period the baby develops a readiness for taking solid foods and begins the process of weaning.

PHYSICAL SYSTEM The ovaries, the testes and the prostate gland and also the womb, the genitals, the kidneys and the bladder.

ENDOCRINE SYSTEM Ovaries/testes

MUSIC The Latin dance, a dance of sensation and pleasure.

ANIMAL TOTEM The Makara, a fabulous mythical beast with the dual characteristics of an alligator with a fish tail

# SVADISTHANA – SWEETNESS

The second 100 days are linked to the second energy centre – the sacral chakra, or Svadisthana, which is a Sanskrit word meaning 'sweetness'. It also means 'my own sweet abode'.

Svadisthana is symbolised by a lotus with six petals and it is situated about five centimetres below the naval in the lower region of the abdomen that lies in front of the sacrum bone of the pelvis.

The awakening of this energy centre begins in the second 100 days, the time leading up to and including the baby's six months. Moving beyond the solidity of the earth and the grounding associated with it, a baby now progresses into a time of change. She moves from the base needs of survival into a period of wanting and feeling.

The element associated with this centre is water. The human body is composed of more than 70 per cent water. Just as the Earth's tides are influenced by the moon and its relationship to the other planets of the Universe, so are we. We are perpetually seeking balance between the highs and the lows – the opposites. We are influenced by the rhythms and the cycles of our biology. Women often menstruate with the rhythm of the full moon, and where there are women living together they will often have their monthly flow and times of fertility simultaneously. We are connected by our cycles, the circadian rhythms that govern our states of waking and sleeping, our times of activity and rest, our mental clarity and our dullness, and our emotional extremes. Water is always in a state of change, and it is always finding its own level. This is the chakra that is about desire and tears. It is the time when a baby develops separateness from her mother and from others. She goes from 'being a *part* of another' to being a person *apart* from another – an individual. This is why a baby in the second 100 days is such a delight. She studies people and objects with keen interest. If she desires something, she will reach for it. If she sees someone eating food near her, she will drool and reach for her share of it.

Svadisthana is the centre of duality, the state of complementary opposites, of pleasure and pain, good and bad, tasty and horrid, 'I want' and 'I reject'. It is the state of freedom that comes with movement and of having choices.

A baby in her second 100 days develops a readiness for the weaning process, which starts with an ability and desire to take solid foods. It is with the weaning process that a baby starts on her true journey as an individual earthling.

While a lot of what has been described in the first 100 days is still happening for the baby in the second 100 days, there are some new signs that become incorporated into or layered over her grounding behaviour. This is because even though your baby has made tremendous advances in becoming grounded, her root energy centre will continue to open further as she learns new skills of survival on earth. As an analogy, she might have skills in the ABC of survival, but from now she will continue to gradually develop and hone those skills and develop higher skills for her survival.

With the stirring of the second chakra in the second 100 days, a baby starts to develop the simple aspects associated with this energy centre while continuing to develop her first chakra. It is important to realise this because a baby's chakras are undeveloped and unprotected. They exist in a form that allows the body to function, particularly in hormone release, but as the energy centres slowly begin to open, certain characteristics of behaviour then begin to manifest.

Physically, this chakra is one of developing new skills. Being able to roll over, use the hands meaningfully, sit with support for a short time, and to vocalise with pleasure and frustration are all skills that develop with her growing ability to have a choice.

Emotionally, Svadisthana is about pleasure, joy, feeling good and deservedness. It is about what we desire, and if we cannot get what we desire then we have feelings of frustration. Desire and frustration – this is a duality. It is about feeling good about one's self. Our wholesome sense of our sexuality, fulfilment and joy and our connection with others arise in this centre.

Mentally, this chakra is where attitudes of *having* and of *being* enough, of life enjoyment, and of wellbeing have their roots. When these attitudes are positive, then we have freedom. This energy centre is where choice begins to grow. Watch a baby with her toys, how her eyes move from one to the other before she makes a choice and reaches out with her hand to grasp it. Ultimately this centre controls our ability to move forward in life. How we see life and its pleasures, how we view our social mores and develop our own sense of ethical behaviour, all arise here in this energy centre. It is also the centre of our imagination and creativity.

Svadisthana is sweetness of life. It is associated with the communion, which comes through close relationships and also through the union of the individual soul with a universal consciousness. This period from 14 to 28 weeks can be one of the most joyful times for your baby and for you. It is a time when new relationships can be forged.

# THE BEHAVIOUR OF A SWEET BABY

## 'I FEEL AND I WANT'

## A consciousness of sensation and pleasure

The second or sacral chakra is the energetic core of a baby's social and creative instincts. This centre enables her to open up to relationships with others. No longer will she exclusively identify himself as part of her mother and she will now be able to have open relationships with others as well as with herself.

The world for a baby of this age, from 14 to 28 weeks, is a wonderful, safe place, with lots of things to look at, touch, taste and explore. When a baby of this age grizzles, it is because she is either hungry or tired or occasionally unwell. Life at this age is not boring!

This is the age of reaching out for the receiving and giving of pleasure. In the beginning of this period, when your baby is about 14 weeks old, she will prefer to be in a cot with plenty of room around her. Allow her arms to be free (not swaddled) so that they can relax out to her side and up near her head. She will love sleeping fully on her back now that she is feeling more secure. Eventually she begins to move around the bed. Trying to keep her snug and covered is almost impossible. This baby loves to kick her legs, and bedclothes too if they are in the way!

She develops a relationship with her toys, or her favourite sheet or blanket and even with her thumb or fingers, which she can turn to for comfort when she is tired or in a stressful situation. She begins to develop preferences. She now belongs to you rather than being a *part* of you. She appreciates your full attention when she is feeding and will become agitated if you are distracted during her feed. Feeding often has to be a quiet contract between you and her, with no interruptions or conversations with anyone else.

Expressions of anger or frustration, excitement or tiredness, are easier to read in her behaviour. When she is tired, this baby begins to lose excitement and eye contact with you. She stops engaging with you and also with her environment. She also develops preferences for different foods and she definitely has a favourite breast!

It is also the time when sex-related differences begin to show some definitude. Infant boys, generally, tend to be more rambunctious and girl babies of this age tend to respond more to emotional situations reflected in facial expressions of people around them.

The sexuality of a baby, present from birth, becomes more exposed. With increased arm and hand control, a baby now develops the ability to touch her own genitals. This is a healthy and normal activity that can be disturbing for some parents, because western societies have been programmed to believe that it is not appropriate behaviour.

Now is a very good time to look at your own attitudes to personal intimacy, to discuss them openly with your partner and, if you are feeling comfortable about it, with your family and your friends. That way you can begin to feel a lot easier about intimacy and can prepare your attitudes for when your baby is older and you can feel quite comfortable about talking to your child about his or her sexuality.

Boy babies have penile erections in the womb, some are born with erections and often they have an erection when they are feeding. Girl babies are known to have vaginal secretions within the first weeks of life, and probably do so when they are still in the womb.

During a nappy change, the facial expression, the reaction and the language of the carer need to be understanding and accepting. If a baby experiences or perceives any signs of disapproval around their genitals at nappy change and bath time, then they will grow up with an understanding that they are not OK, and that they are *definitely* not OK in the region below the belly button.

A baby derives pleasure through her body. Massaging and cuddling nourishes body and soul and also enables a child to feel good about herself. Eventually a child learns to nurture others in the same way, growing into adulthood with a healthy attitude to their own sexuality and respecting the needs and boundaries of others, including their own children.

Self-respect and self-love begin to blossom here in the second chakra. Babies and children are very vulnerable and need to be nurtured and guarded with loving vigilance, particularly during this period. It is important that a child is never taken advantage of, touched inappropriately or treated as though any part of their body or bodily function is dirty or shameful. A carer's positive facial expression during happy changes is very important. The development of this energy centre requires the greatest of respect in childhood and throughout a person's entire life.

# TIRED SIGNS

The tired signs of a baby from 14 to 28 weeks of age become a lot easier to read, not only because her communication is more open but also because you began to recognise her signs in the first 100 days and you are beginning to understand your child's behaviour.

Here are the signs that indicate tiredness in a baby during a baby's second 100 days:

**Yawning:** At this age a baby's lungs are becoming softer, more flexible and inflatable, and she is able to breath more deeply. Consequently there are not as many yawns as in her first three months, so when you see one it is more likely to be a genuine sign of tiredness.

**Flailing agitated arm movements:** Rather than measured and co-ordinated movements, a baby in her second 100 days will begin to 'flap' her arms like a bird, one arm at a time. She also loses interest in her toys.

**Loss of eye-contact:** This is a subtle process, but is more noticeable just before she begins to grizzle and stiffen.

**Heel digging:** Usually into the surface she is lying on while arching her back. A baby at this age, when she is relaxed and fresh, loves to have her legs in the air and to play with her toes and to try to pull her socks off her feet. As she begins to tire, one leg will lower and push into the surface on which she is lying so that she can arch her back. Eventually both legs will rest down and you will notice other tired signs.

**The grizzle:** This is a familiar tired sign by now. Even older children and parents and grandmas grizzle and whinge and get cranky when they are tired. And they are definitely not as sweet as they were a short moment ago.

**Self-comforting:** Reaching for her favourite comfort – thumb, fingers, blanket, wrap or toy.

**Rubbing her face:** into your shoulder or the soft surface on which she is lying.

**Flicking or pulling at ears and the back of the head:** This is a very good tired sign.

**Rubbing eyes:** Baby will rub at eyes with fists.

**Being loud:** Baby becomes vocally louder.

As soon as tired signs happen, it is time for a baby to go to bed. The longer the delay, then the more difficult it is for her to be able to settle herself, and consequently there will be more crying and more distress for those hearing her de-stress.

From the beginning of this second 100 days, a baby sleeps better if she has the freedom of a cot rather than a crib. It is also a safer option, because this is the time when a baby learns to roll over, and if she sleeps on a firm clean mattress, she does not come to harm. She may get herself caught in a corner or pushed up against the head of the cot but she will call out to you to come and help her to get comfortable.

The cot needs to be clear of doonas or duvets, large toys and bumpers. One or two small soft hand toys are ideal to have in her bed and while she is fairly settled she will remain tucked in with a sheet and blankets.

The soles of the feet are covered with cells that are temperature sensors. It is very difficult for us to sleep peacefully when our feet are cold. This applies to a baby also. If a baby is not sleeping well, it is probably because her feet and legs are cold. Simply wearing socks can solve this. This depends on climatic conditions, the warmth of a baby's environment and whether she feels the cold. Understanding temperature patterns of the local region can help a parent to analyse a baby's sleeping patterns.

A baby often feels cold and wakes for a feed of warming milk at about 4 am, because the coldest part of the night comes just before the approaching dawn.

A good guide for clothing a baby is to dress her in layers, and for her to be dressed in one layer more than what you yourself are wearing. Sleeping in the same bed with the warmth of another person is regarded as one layer, and if you sleep under a doona, check on what thickness of layers it is equivalent to.

Tucking a baby in with a sheet is a good signal for her that it is time for sleep, but most babies in their second 100 days will kick their way from under any covers. If she is experiencing the cold, then make sure she is dressed in a singlet, socks and all-in-one suit and placed in a recommended sleeping bag that has sleeves so that her movements won't leave her uncovered during the night.

A baby often perspires and feels hot to touch shortly after she goes to sleep for the night. This happens because her body is releasing the excess heat that it has accumulated during his stimulating day. There is no reason for concern about this, but be sure to monitor her and make any adjustments if her body temperature remains high.

# CRYING

Babies nearly always cry when they are tired.

Tired crying starts with grizzling, which grows louder and more intense the more tired and uncomfortable she becomes.

A baby will also cry or be irritable and grizzly when she is hungry. However in this period from 14 to 28 weeks, most babies will develop a definite feeding routine and a sleeping pattern that follows on from this. Consequently there is not as much crying. Also a baby of this age is quite vocal and beginning to be a lot more physically active. This vocalising and moving around allows the baby to blow off steam, which she then doesn't need to release through crying. Some babies however may need to routinely wind down with some crying, sometimes for as long as 10 to 15 minutes just before they go to sleep, and this can happen before each sleep period.

A baby may also cry out when she has a sudden fright or hurt, and she will need some good cuddling and soothing in order to calm down.

As the second 100 days initiates the development of the sacral chakra, which is the energy centre of duality and relationships with others, a baby in this stage of development will gradually become aware of separation from her parent and other familiar faces. She will often feel unsettled if she is tired and her parent is not in view and, while at this age it is very transitory, it is the beginning of the condition known as 'separation anxiety'. This can cause some crying, although at this age it does not last for long.

A baby is a lot more unsettled if she becomes chronically tired, which is the type of tiredness that builds up over days or weeks, particularly if she is overstressed (has been on a journey or has had an illness), has had days of inadequate sleep, or if she is over stimulated (there have been houseguests, or a baby is 'kept up' until a parent gets home from work). This chronic state can lead to a very grizzly, tense and crying baby. The only way that this type of tiredness can be dealt with is through crying, in order to let the body release the tension.

Sleep masks the condition temporarily, but generally a baby who is *chronically* tired does not sleep well. She has short cycles of sleep and her nights are often disturbed, and consequently the whole family does not sleep adequately. This situation can be alleviated with a week of 'staying at home', very little stimulation, and a baby being put to her bed as soon as she has had her feed. There will also be quite a bit of crying to be released, but most parents who have had this situation for a few days generally feel that at the end of the process they have a much happier and contented baby. It is worth the 'pain' of the crying process.

There is a modern tendency to allow a baby to have 'up' time or playtime for about an hour and a half after her feed, but this tends to lead to settling difficulties, because when food reaches the upper parts of the gut fairly shortly after the end of the meal there is a neuro-transmitting (or nerve signal) process that tells the brain to sleep. If a baby does not have the opportunity to sleep when this neuro-chemical process happens, then this lost sleep leads to chronic tiredness. That is why the option of playtime can be better *before* her meal.

A sleeping routine is set out in the section on feeding, because both sleeping and feeding routines provide a good rest pattern when they are considered together.

# FEEDING

Sometime in the period from four to seven months, a baby develops a readiness for solid food. For a baby who is exclusively breast fed, this is the beginning of the weaning process.

Because of the increasing incidence of asthma, there is a tendency to delay the introduction of foods apart from breast milk or formula until six months of age. Therefore, even though there is behavioural readiness for solid foods, it is a matter of choice when it is introduced. The choice can be made depending on the baby's family history of allergies, and in consultation with a paediatrician, family doctor or the community nurse.

There are three signs that a baby is ready for solid foods:

- Baby's weight gain pattern tends to plateau or to slow. However, it is a normal pattern for weight gain to be less than the dramatic weight gains of the first 100 days.
- Baby will show great interest in anybody else eating food, and in fact will begin to lean forward, with a good deal of anticipation and excitement, for her 'share'.
- Baby will begin to wake for an extra feed at night. This last sign is not a lot of fun for her mother, particularly when there have been two to four weeks of sleeping 'through the night'.

These three signs tend to start at the end of baby's first 100 days. That is why it is the parent's choice, depending on the signs and also family history, when 'solids' are introduced, somewhere between four to six months of age. While taking in and swallowing solids is a new way of taking foods, the action also develops the muscles needed for the development of speech.

# The introduction of solid foods

It is believed that motor development, or movement development, is not programmed into the brain from birth. It is stimulated by a baby's exploration and desire to master new tasks. This behaviour is influenced by a maturing central nervous system and the body's abilities with new movements. The support of the baby's environment to develop and practise these new skills becomes very necessary in the second 100 days.

Svadisthana is the energy centre of movement and creativity and it is also the centre which represents the sense of taste – a very appropriate time to start thinking of new foods and new ways of exploring them.

At four months of age, a baby's readiness for solid food becomes very apparent. The tongue thrust reflex, when the tongue is used for sucking, tends to be weaker than it was at birth, when a baby's survival depended on her ability to suck at the nipple. Now she begins to put everything into her mouth. This activity has a lot to do with her learning about eating solid foods, but it is also how she learns about the shapes and textures of things, because her tongue is more sensitive to shapes and textures than her fingers are at the beginning of the second 100 days. Gradually this changes over the next three to four months as the fingers become more co-ordinated and sensitive to change and her ability to discern visual differences becomes more developed.

A baby's responsiveness to taste is very similar to an adult's, which suggests that taste preferences are innate. A baby will let you know what she thinks of certain tastes – her facial expressions and her ability to relish or refuse what tastes and textures are offered her are very obvious. But here is a conundrum. A baby can absolutely love something for two or three weeks then have a complete turn around and refuse this particular offering for the next month. This is not a concern because the sacral chakra creates a sense of duality and opposites and her sudden switch in what she likes or what she refuses is not permanent. Be patient and offer these tastes in another four to six weeks.

## Suggested routine for introduction of solids

Milk is the most important food for a baby under six months, so solids are offered straight after the breast feed, or half way through the bottle of formula.

For a baby six months and over, milk is not as important as her solid foods, so offer the solids before the breast or bottle feed. She may only feed at one breast or will not finish all her formula, but some of the milk from her bottle will also have been used for mixing with her cereal.

Introduce a new fruit or vegetable only every three or four days. This will reveal any food intolerances and also gradually build up a full palate of vegetables and fruits. Delay offering strawberries or citrus or tomatoes for the first year as they commonly cause food sensitivity reactions. Stew or steam all stone fruits. Avocado or banana can be mashed and given without cooking.

It is good to think of a feeding routine in terms of breakfast, early lunch, afternoon tea and dinner, with a sleep as soon as the meal is over. Playtime can come before the baby eats.

A suggested meal replacement routine would be to introduce solid food gradually over 3 weeks as in table below:

| WEEK 1 | Dinnertime (5.00-7.00 pm):<br>Rice cereal (1 teaspoonful) mixed with some expressed breast milk |
|---|---|
| WEEK 2 | Breakfast (6.30-8.00 am):<br>Rice cereal mixed with milk and pureed fruit<br>Dinnertime (5.00-7.00 pm):<br>Rice cereal mixed with expressed breast milk, formula or cool boiled water. |
| WEEK 3 | Breakfast (as for week 2)<br>Lunch (11.00-11.30 am):<br>Steamed vegetables can be cooked and frozen in iceblock trays then emptied into a plastic bag or container and kept in the freezer. Try pumpkin or sweet potato to start with and offer one iceblock cube portion. |

This routine also will bring the baby into a family pattern. However it needs to be remembered that this is a solids routine, and breast or bottle may need to be offered at other times (early morning and supper – making five or six milk feeds) while the quantities of solids are gradually increased.

## Suggested feeding routine after six months

After six months of age, milk is not as important as solid food, and the amounts of milk required and taken by an infant gradually decrease over the second six months.

From six months of age, a baby requires 600 to 700 mls of *milk product* per day. Milk product includes breast milk, formula, milk used in cooking, yoghurt, cheese and soya products, such as soy milk, and curds such as tofu. Once she reaches the age of one year she will require only 500 ml milk product per day

# A suggested fee1ding routine for a child over six months of age:

| | |
|---|---|
| 5.00 - 6.30 am | Breast or bottle feed (150 ml)<br>Back to bed. |
| 7.00 - 8.00 am | Breakfast: cereal, fruit, yoghurt<br>Breast/bottle feed if there was no milk feed before 6.30 am. |
| 8.30 - 9.00 am | Back to bed. Surprisingly this is often a long sleep,<br>even though the baby has slept well through the night. |
| 11.00 - 11.30 am | Lunch, which is the main meal of the day: chicken, meat<br>(and towards the end of the first year, fish) and vegetables.<br>Offer sips of cool boiled water from a cup throughout the lunchtime feed, because vegetables can be fairly gluggy, and babies will often stop eating the meal, not because they have had enough but because they need to moisten their mouth. If a baby finishes her meal consistently, then increase the amounts. Offer the breast or formula at the end of the meal (this is often the first milk feed that a baby will wean herself from, so don't be alarmed if she refuses milk). |
| 12.30 - 1.00 pm | Back to bed for afternoon sleep. |
| 2.30 - 3.30 pm | Afternoon tea. This is a milk substitute meal – yoghurt or custard with fruit<br>Sips of water if required |
| 4.00 - 4.30 pm | To bed for short nap, 20 to 30 minutes<br>Some babies need this nap to get them through to dinner. Most babies are fairly grizzly and tired by this time of the day. Some babies will not have this nap. |
| 5.00 - 6.00 pm | Dinner.<br>This can be a carbohydrate meal, as carbohydrate takes longer to digest and provides the energy to last through the night. Therefore, offer pasta, rice or couscous, with any sauces or favourite foods added, particularly cheese. It is also a good opportunity to offer hard-boiled egg yolk, which is rich in iron and other nutrients. However the egg white is withheld from a baby's diet until she is one year old because of the risk of egg white allergy. |

Because milk is not as important as solids for a child over six months, it is given at the end of the meal and is also included in cooking of the food.

This feeding routine is a good daytime one for a working mother who wishes to continue breast feeding. This is because milk is not absolutely necessary at the lunchtime feed, and milk can be given in other forms such as yoghurt, custard and cheese. However this routine takes a few weeks to build up to, because it is still necessary to leave three to four days between offering a new food to a baby. This is done so any food intolerances can be determined without confusion of 'which' food.

Throughout the day a baby may need sips of water, particularly if the weather is warm and dry.

## A BABY ON THE MOVE

The development of Svadisthana marks the beginnings of co-ordinated and deliberate movements that are born of a baby's desire to explore her surroundings and all things in them.

When she is supine (lying on her back), at about four and a half months of age, she raises her head from the surface on which she is lying – bringing her chin towards her chest. She moves her limbs vigorously and reaches out for toys.

At five months she lifts her legs to vertical, and at about five and a half months she will grasp her feet and explore them – sometimes with her mouth. At this time she stretches out her arms to be lifted up. When she is helped to a sitting position, she braces her shoulders and assists. Her head is well controlled, her back is straighter and she can sit with support. Held in a sitting position, she can bounce vigorously.

When she is prone (on her tummy), she gradually lifts her head and chest higher until at six months she can support herself on her open palms with extended arms stretched out in front of her.

Between four to six months, she rolls over front to back (this may happen earlier) and at about six and a half months she can roll from back to front. Once a baby has managed this she can roll across a room, and from this position she will begin to lift her bottom in her first attempts to crawl.

From the age of seven months, she can pull herself up to sit while in her pram, and she can sit on the floor with the support of her own arms.

So it can be seen that this baby, through the awakening of Svadisthana, is beginning to explore movement in order to satisfy her desire for something by reaching out to it. Some babies in this time may become frustrated in their efforts to achieve whatever it is that they want and will yell with annoyance – they need help and understanding until their gross motor skills have caught up. It is an emotional time for her, and her frustration can last for a few weeks. Without her desire for exploration and for getting what she wants, her gross motor skills would not develop. She is driven by desire.

As a baby is beginning to move in the second 100 days, her environment needs to be secure and safe so that she does not come to harm. If she wants something that is not safe, then she needs to be distracted with another activity or object. If she has possession of something that is not right for her, then offer her something else while you remove the object from her. She is easily distracted, because the world is so attractive for her.

Babies at this age are very trusting of their environment. As their guardians we must make their environment safe for them. We always need to think one step ahead of a baby, and make her environment safe for her next stage of development.

Stairs require barricades top and bottom, cupboards need childproof catches and treasures need to be placed out of reach. Hot drinks, such as your cup of tea, need to be up high and out of reach, and obvious dangerous objects removed. What was once exclusively your home is now your baby's home.

While your baby is fairly immobile, take the opportunity to do a 'safe home audit', for once a baby is on the move there is no stopping her. She is going to travel off her rug, across the room and down the hallway before you know it. The world is her oyster.

# TRAVELLING

The second 100 days is a wonderful age for a baby to travel with her family.

In some cases families need to travel overseas or interstate to visit their relatives, so long air flights may be necessary for all the family to meet the new addition. This can mean travelling through time zones, having no access to food preparation or adequate bathing facilities. A baby doesn't really care, and if her parents are flexible and relaxed then the journey can be easily undertaken.

A baby in this age period becomes a very sociable and curious person. She is willing to give big broad smiles to anyone who smiles and talks with her. She is not yet on the move, her sleeps through the night and, as long as her family is with her, she is happy and flexible. She will sleep anywhere, be happy to sit on a comfy lap and play in any situation.

It is a lot easier for a breastfed infant and her mother. If she has already commenced on solid foods, then she needs to have been introduced to commercial baby foods. For a formula-fed baby, travelling can be made easy by travelling with her bottles full of cool boiled water. These can be easily heated in restaurants, hotel rooms and on planes and trains, and formula powder added just before the feed.

Travelling can be a thirsty business so every baby needs to travel with bottles of cool boiled water for quenching thirst between feeds.

Travelling is tiring, and while a baby can usually sleep fairly well during the journey, she will still build up chronic tiredness because of extra handling, stimulation and sharing the family's excitement and tensions. This tiredness can be sorted out when she reaches her destination through some crying and a bit more time in bed on the first day of the baby's holiday in order for her to discharge her tenseness and stress that has built up during the journey. Once this is achieved she will then settle into her usual routine.

This is an easier process if holiday hosts understand that the crying is not permanent, but is part of the travelling process for a baby. It also means that the baby will be much happier and more responsive to new people in her life, once she has yelled out her tense tiredness.

# PARENTING WITH DELIGHT

Parenting in the second 100 days can be the most delightful time for new parents. All the anxiety of the first three months seems to disappear and new strength comes.

This is when a mother's body returns to pre-pregnancy state. At about four to five months the enhanced growth of a woman's hair and nails slows down – most mothers notice shedding of hair, which can be alarming, but this is the body shedding the extra hair that grew in pregnancy.

Although the breasts return to a softness that existed before pregnancy in readiness for the baby's reduced need for milk after six months, the supply remains adequate. As this is the time of weaning the baby to solid food and a lesser number of breast feeds, it is also when the menstrual cycle returns and the body is prepared to undergo another pregnancy. This is, after all, the time of Svadisthana, the centre of creativity.

Rather than trying to survive sleepless nights, parents can now get on the move and return to a lifestyle that was there before the days of having a new baby. Rejuvenating and recreating a partnership between parents – two people who have just undertaken an amazing birth journey – can be made with joy and desire. Sheer love of a child, mutually shared between two people, can move a couple into a new direction of adventure and exploration and a new mature love for each other. Life is never static. It is forever evolving. Now develops new sensuality, new desires and new dreams. And if there's a new dress (especially if it's orange), put it on, book the babysitter and step out for some Latin dancing.

Fall in love with each other again. Buy flowers and chocolates for each other, and eat by candlelight. It is worth the effort and your baby will reflect your love and contentedness.

The sacral chakra determines our physical ability to move forward in life and it is influenced by our attitudes about pleasure and a sense of our own sensuality. If it hasn't already returned, then you may find that your sexual desire is rekindled and, through this, emotional growth is ensured through new fulfilment, joy and a new connectedness with each other and with friends and family.

The first 100 days of being a new parent can be very challenging with emotions bouncing all over the place. There is also a very strong desire to 'get on top of things' need to 'get on top of things'. So in the second 100 days, it is really time to have pleasure in your life. If you find that it is not happening for you, then share this with your partner and also seek someone to counsel you to help you find the joy, health and pleasure that is your right at this stage of parenting.

A baby will always express what a parent, particularly her mother, is holding within herself. So if your baby is tearful, cranky and unsettled, maybe look inside yourself and find the part of you that is tearful and unhappy. A baby is a great emotional barometer, intuitively picking up all sorts of signals and relaying them.

Svadisthana means sweetness. It also translates as 'my own sweet abode' which means that it is the very innermost parts of us that provide our own solace – a place where it is pleasurable to go to find peace and contentedness. If we have temporarily lost our way to this inner place, then discontent and frustration builds up and, if not addressed, festers and erupts and damages not only our own self but also our loved ones. Learning to love ourselves and to be grateful for what we have releases much of this feeling.

Practical counselling and being part of a parenting group can help us to gain balance in our life. Taking up some form of physical exercise such as yoga, dance or other movement loosens up the pelvis and releases tensions. Walking is free and liberating, and can be done with your baby in a pram or sling. Walk with your partner or a friend.

Meditation releases the spirit and helps to bring peace. Meditation also can bring insight into your life and lead the way to compassion and self-loving, to be true to yourself and be appropriate with others.

It is very easy at this stage of parenting to slip into the role of being a martyr to our family and children – leaving our own needs to last. This can build up a resentment that seems to quietly rumble away behind every action – '*What about me?*' This can become a life of suffering, where a martyr can relinquish all claim to personal happiness to the detriment of mental and emotional health and physical wellbeing. Life becomes a sacrifice, which in modern western cultures has been seen as a virtue.

If we continually deny our own needs, what can our children learn from us? When we deny our own needs, we stop growing and expanding and taking in new ideas of the world and of our life. And through doing this there is sown the idea that others should do the same, especially our children.

Creating a life of self-sacrifice also closes down our creativity in other areas. We encourage children to be creative and to watch their growth through their achievements. We need to hold the same vision for ourselves, to turn our dreams into realities and even though little children have no true concept of anyone else's emotional needs before the age of seven or eight, they can be guided towards that understanding through seeing their parents as happy and creative people who are having fun in their life.

In this second 100 days, it is time to reclaim the Emperor/Empress in us, to be prepared to receive as well as to give. Try to do something really nice for yourself every day of your life, and make it a gift to yourself. This will provide the foundation for building the self-worth that is to be further developed in the next 100 days.

*Desire is a combination of pleasure and the urge to individuate.*

CARL GUSTAV JUNG

# THE THIRD
# 100 DAYS

# MANIPURA
## *The Solar Plexus Chakra*

# INTRODUCTION

The third energy centre Manipura, situated in the upper abdomen in the region of the solar plexus and therefore regarded as the solar plexus chakra, is represented by ten petals and awakens in the baby between seven and ten months of age. Manipura is a Sanskrit word meaning 'lustrous gem'.

This chakra relates to strength and confirmation, and the assertion of self will.

A baby, in his first 100 days becomes grounded. He is fairly inert and there is not much movement. In his second 100 days his emotions begin to flow and he becomes far more adaptable. Now, in his third 100 days, he moves into a development and expression of his power, his will and his energy. This is the time when you will notice that he is becoming an individual, becoming far more dynamic and determined to go in the direction that *he* wants to go. This little person is not nearly as compliant as he used to be!

Alchemy was an ancient art practised in the middle ages. It grew out of a belief that base metals could be transformed into gold. The fundamental concept of alchemy stemmed from the philosopher Aristotle's doctrine that all things tend to reach perfection. The concept of alchemy is a wonderful way to understand change and its different stages of growth in all areas of our life.

The third 100 days of a baby's life mark the beginning of moving beyond a feeling of deep unity with his mother to forging a relationship with himself and satisfying the need to have some command over his environment. He will often reach out for food and indicate other needs through developing clear gestures and even words. Gestures are the basics of motor, verbal and social skills.

It is from this third energy centre, Manipura, that we become warriors. Life becomes a mission, wherein the self sets off on a journey of exploration and discovery. This is the centre of self-esteem – feeling good about ourselves and our ideas.

# The Third Energy Centre

MANIPURA

'Lustrous gem'

## *The Lotus of Ten Petals*

The Third 100 Days
Self-worth and Personal Power

COLOUR: Yellow, an energetic colour that radiates light and warmth. The brightest colour of the spectrum, it focuses attention, attracts new ideas and is flexible and adaptable. Yellow has self-control, style and sophistication. It gives off a feeling of wellbeing – people generally feel good when surrounded by bright, sunny yellow.

MUSIC: The march, originally created to stimulate and organize the movements of large groups of people, particularly soldiers. Marching enables us to feel powerful. It is the music of action and of movement.

SENSE: Vision, the inner sight that we develop with our intuition. Insight arises from our gut feelings and leads to 'right' action.

PHYSICAL BODY: The digestive system – stomach, liver, large and small intestines and pancreas.

ENDOCRINE GLAND: The pancreas and adrenal medulla.

ANIMAL TOTEM: The ram, head of the flock, creating and building the group, but quite capable of battering down walls and gates. The ram's penetrative power is always ambivalent – it fecundates and creates, and yet it wounds and destroys.

# MANIPURA – POWER

The third energy centre, Manipura, is symbolised by a lotus flower of ten petals and is governed by the element fire. Fire is the most volatile of the elements. It is hot and dry and masculine and active. The body's natural fire, the digestion of food, is the way that the body nourishes itself.

Physically, Manipura is situated in the region of the solar plexus, the network of nerves situated just below the diaphragm. Its name, solar, implies that here is the fire of the body. This energy centre rules the metabolic system – its role is to regulate and distribute metabolic energy throughout the body. The nerves of the solar plexus feed the stomach, the liver, the spleen, the small intestine and the kidney. It is in these organs that the processes of digestion and filtering of waste take place. It is also in this region that we are sensitive to situations – where we have our 'gut' feelings. This is where we have 'fire in the belly', the knowing that we 'can achieve', and the courage to 'make it all happen'. It is in the solar plexus chakra that the desires of the second energy centre and the love of the heart centre find the *action* for manifestation.

The gland associated with the third energy centre is the pancreas. The pancreas is a long soft organ that lies near the stomach and, in response to nerve and hormonal mechanisms, secretes juices and enzymes into the intestine to aid digestion and the absorption of nutrients. The pancreas also secretes hormones directly into the bloodstream, one of which is insulin, which lowers blood sugar levels, and another is glucagon, which raises them. These processes are derived from the transformation of food into the energy necessary for sustaining life and growth.

Living food contains prana or life force. We take in this life force or energy when we eat fresh foods, the organs of digestion distribute this energy and the solar plexus chakra distributes spiritual energy throughout the body. When food is prepared with positive and loving energy then that energy gets distributed to anyone who eats the food. If the food is polluted with negative energy, then that energy is passed on to all who eat it. Laura Esquivel wrote a beautiful book *Like Water for Chocolate* which illustrates this well.

On an emotional level Manipura revolves around power. This power is that which we draw on in order to act on our ideas and desires. Inappropriate use of this power to control or dominate another person is an indication that this energy centre is out of balance and overactive, and often is an indication of low self-esteem.

The emotions of power reflect our relationship to inner strength and self-worth, which enable us to take a stand for ourselves. Being comfortable with our own power allows us to act with confidence and to exercise freedom of choice in most matters. If we are not comfortable with our right to our own power then we avoid situations that call for an affirmative response, we find it difficult to say 'no' and to stand firm for our own rights. Childhood is a difficult time to achieve this – little children are surrounded by authority figures who direct their lives – and it is not until adolescence that this chakra is truly able to assert itself and come into full expression.

Mentally, Manipura holds thoughts of our power, our confidence and freedom of choice. When we do not value ourselves, then our ideas of our own power can be under- or over-expressed in relationship to others. When we are comfortable with our self then we are careful how we use our power and nurture the way that we are free to make that choice of what is right for us. This centre is concerned with the rational, logical and factual aspects of our thinking. It reflects our personal sense of control – or lack of it. It also manifests our creative vision.

Spiritually, Manipura brings us instinctual knowing, our 'gut feeling', our core inner knowing about others and situations that we encounter. Because it is such an active energy, our lesson in life is to develop peace and wisdom in how we use our power and to learn to stay true to our self. We learn how to transform our thoughts and the actions that respond to those thoughts. This is how we can modify our behaviour and teach our children to do the same.

This is particularly true of this chakra, because it is from this energy centre that our attitudes and values can mature and be reflected in our actions. We can find here the strength to resist forces outside of us, such as peer pressure or media marketing designed to make us feel that we are somehow lacking. When we fail to love ourselves, we tend to submit to these outside forces, thinking that if we do then we will be more loveable and happy and satisfied. Building and strengthening our own self-worth from this centre enables us to stand strong and to grow spiritually. Knowing that we are entitled to a good life allows abundance to come to us.

Denying our own worth leads us down a path to giving away our power. We lose the ability to say 'no', and end up becoming a drudge unable to stand up for our rights. This is reflected at a physical level in how we nurture ourselves with good food, good sleep and a healthy active lifestyle that nourishes our soul.

This is the centre of self-esteem – of creating a healthy and strong relationship with the self.

It is in this energy centre where we struggle with our own character, just as Hercules did when he overcame the Nemean lion, an enormous beast with a pelt proof against iron, bronze and stone. When Hercules reached Nemea, he could not find anyone to direct him to the lion because the lion had already destroyed the population. It was only through Hercules' own searching that he found and confronted the beast and overcame it (the symbolic struggle with his own reflection or shadow) by seizing it with his bare hands. This myth reveals the victory of the human soul over its own weaknesses that reside within the ego.

This is how we become our own powerful warriors of self-transformation. We learn to face ourselves, to look within, and to recognise and own the parts of us that we suppress. In this way we acknowledge them. Only then can we recognise and strengthen the goodness and talent within us.

Manipura truly opens during adolescence, but it is in the years of infancy and early childhood that feelings of power and impotence start to stir. One has only to observe the behaviour of a two-year-old child to see these two opposing forces in full action. At ten months of age, a baby has a concept of the word 'no', and with this understanding comes testing of his power. Once he is on the move he is beginning to act on his right of choice.

# THE BEHAVIOUR OF A
# SELF-WILLED BABY
## 'I CAN', 'I WILL'

The third energy centre or solar plexus chakra is the energetic core of an infant's *will* to act. It enables him to move towards childhood and to become an individual, free to make his own choices and to act on them. If he is carefully and lovingly guided to be a powerful and effective individual then he can grow up to be a balanced and powerful adult in full charge of himself and his actions.

Biologically, this time for a baby is one of change, particularly in the development of his fine motor skills (such as precise finger movements), as well as the gross motor skills of walking and the social skills associated with the development and understanding of language.

Emotionally, it is the time for being aware of distance and separation, as he begins to move away physically from the parent, though still having a great need to have the parent nearby and often in sight.

A child of this age wants to have more control over his environment. It is often in this period that a infant can suddenly wean himself from the breast completely and want control over how he has his food. He wants to be in charge of the action – directing the spoon and contents himself! This autonomous behaviour can be quite a challenge for parents, particular as the food often ends up all over the floor. However a baby in this period becomes very affectionate with kisses and cuddles.

Physically, the third 100 days show changes in body proportions and stature in preparation for becoming a toddler. Neurologically, a baby develops from head to limbs. Development of the hands and arms occur in the four-to-seven month period and leg and foot growth and development happen from seven months on. At seven months of age an infant can sit with the support of his own arms and for brief periods can sit unaided. At eight months, he can sit unaided with a good straight back and with an ability to swivel from side to side and to lean forward to reach for a toy without losing his balance.

At eight or nine months, a baby's fine motor skills, such as ability with fingers and thumbs, become more sophisticated. He is now able to pick up a fine piece of fluff from the carpet with thumb and index finger opposed.

Mentally, a baby of about nine months develops a concept of 'object permanence', which is the knowing that an object hasn't 'gone' even though it is out of sight. Life becomes experimentation and observation. Dropping an object from a height (generally from the highchair at feed times!) and watching how it falls is great fun. This is all part of learning about his environment and his place within it.

It is also at mealtimes that a baby will explore and control his feeding. Often, anything delivered by a spoon in someone else's control is rejected and having finger food becomes the only way that a baby will eat.

Socially, wariness of strangers develops at the same time and a baby can feel quite invaded if 'rushed' by anyone he is not sure about. He needs to observe for quite a while before interacting with a stranger or a family member outside his immediate and known circle. This is known as person permanence and it is how an infant learns to discriminate and to protect himself from strangers. Communication is usually by gesture and some babies in this period develop a word or two.

Using syllables with both a consonant and a vowel is usual and repetitive, though often there will not be meaning attached to them. It is a repetitive 'talking' and a great joy to dad because usually the first syllable is da-da or bub-bub. Mum-mum comes a bit later!

Spiritually, this time marks the beginning of baby's unique character and revealing more of his personality. It is also the time of the development of action, self-will and self-awareness.

# Tired Signs

**Grizzling:** The grizzle is here to stay for about the next seven or eight years and could probably be put alongside 'bad' behaviour.

**Loudness:** If his chattering becomes louder and more persistent and guttural, rather than a sweet talking, it is a sign that this infant is feeling ready for sleep.

**Yawning:** Yawning as a tired sign is lessening in frequency and can be easily missed at this age. It usually accompanies other tired signs.

**Blowing rubber lips:** The soft raspberry snorts like those made by a horse. This is a tired sign to listen for rather than having to observe.

**Biting:** The human body becomes tense when it is tired. One area of tension is the jaw. Because women tend to continually discharge their tension with talking, jaw tension is not as evident; however for men who do not discharge their tension vocally, a lot of tension builds up around the temporo-mandibular joint. Babies also have this build up and to relieve this tension they will burrow their head into the shoulder of whoever is holding them, open their mouth and clamp it tight around that shoulder. It hurts. (In fact it can bruise the shoulder, but bring relief for the baby.) This is not naughtiness, so scolding is not always appropriate. It is tiredness, and a sign that the baby needs to sleep.

**Arching back and stiffening of the legs:** This is another sign of tension in the baby, particularly if the baby is not yet on the move. If the infant is on the move he becomes more uncoordinated and accident-prone. This is often when bumps and bruises happen.

**Rubbing eyes:** A very good sign of tiredness at this age. Some babies will also develop redness or circles around the eyes and, just by observing a baby's face, a parent can see the tiredness.

**Flicking or pulling at ears and the back of the head:** This is a very good tired sign. The occasional, very tired baby who has sensitive skin can develop redness and skin roughness if this sign is not recognised. Once the back of the head becomes rough and red then itchiness may mask this sign.

**Searching for comfort – fingers, thumb, wrap or toy:** Usually this comfort searching is the first sign of tiredness, and becomes a gesture of communication.

**'Bad behaviour':** Any infant behaviour that is becoming an irritation for the rest of the family is due to either tiredness or illness. This sign never really goes away. It lasts well into adulthood. Even grandparents can be fairly impossible when they are tired or sick. We just don't cope well with life situations when we are either tired or unwell.

# CRYING

A child in his third 100 days will cry when he becomes tired.

A baby will also grizzle and cry if he is not well. A carer needs to be able to recognise the difference, and at first it is not always apparent. If a well-fed baby is grizzly and unhappy then he is tired.

Some babies at this age still need to cry for up to ten minutes to unwind before falling asleep. This pattern becomes obvious if this infant is happy for the rest of the day.

The period from seven to about ten and a half months is about change and this applies to a baby's eating, sleeping and awake time patterns as well as the achieving of milestones. At this age, a baby will not tolerate or sleep with a dirty nappy. Consequently, if he is in his bed, probably playing happily, and does not settle to sleep as usual, he will become so tired that he will start to cry for a nappy change so that he can settle and sleep.

Crying and grizzling and difficult behaviour also come with hunger, due to low blood sugar levels. Offering sugary food can accentuate this – it just provides a quick sugar hit and then a sudden withdrawal or let down – back to grizzling and crying and more difficult behaviour.

# SLEEPING

A baby of seven months can still have two or three day sleeps and one long night sleep. A baby of ten months may often only have one or two daytime sleeps and one long night sleep. So it can be seen that sleeping patterns can change quite a lot in this period. While the typical sleep requirement for a baby seven to ten months old is on average 14 hours in the 24 hours, it is the night sleep that extends and the day sleeps that shorten, with the second daytime sleep for some babies being dropped every two or three days. This depends on the individual infant and it really depends on the baby's carer being able to read his tired signs.

There is little point in keeping a baby from sleep if he is thoroughly miserable and grizzly. If he is not sleeping enough *for him* during the daytime hours, then he will have a disturbed nighttime sleep (and, consequently, so will her parents). The family becomes irritable and resentful, and this in itself is transferred to the baby. A baby will always express what his parent, particularly his mother, holds within herself and does not express. And thus is set up a cycle of sleeplessness and miserable communication within the family.

Nearly always at this age, the best daytime sleep that a baby has is the sleep that comes after breakfast, which is surprising considering he has just had such a long nighttime sleep. By ten months, this sleep becomes shorter and the afternoon sleep may become longer in readiness for a baby to develop a pattern of one daytime sleep in the afternoon and a slightly longer night sleep. This happens sometime in the second year when he is a toddler, but there is the occasional baby who will develop this pattern towards the end of his first year.

It is important, if a baby is to be a happy baby, for us to understand that if he achieves enough sleep for his needs during the daytime (and that he is adequately fed during the day, and he has learnt to put himself to sleep without any aids, such as rocking, patting, feeding or the dummy), then he will sleep through the night for about 11 hours.

Sleep begets sleep.

Baby also needs to have warm legs and feet, because he will not sleep with cold feet nor will he stay covered in his bed. So dress him adequately to sleep uncovered.

A baby of this age needs two or three small soft toys in bed and some small soft books at the foot of the bed. He will 'read' or entertain himself until he is ready for sleep, and 'read' when he wakes up. If he doesn't have this option available, then he will probably wake you very early in the morning, and what a lot of fun you will all be expected to have!

## FEEDING

A baby in the third 100 days learns to be an independent eater. He wants to be in control of his food. So at about eight or nine months of age he might begin to reject food on a spoon that is offered by another. This baby needs a spoon of his own, lots of finger food and a lot of distraction. A toy at mealtime is often a distraction that will enable whoever is feeding him to sneak in a spoonful of food.

This baby also needs to have a feeding cup of cool boiled water within reach to that he can reach for it and, with help, have sips of water throughout the meal. If he is becoming disinterested in his meal, then offer him a sip of water. It usually leads to him taking in more food. When a baby of this age has 'had enough', he will refuse to take more food and him communication is very clear. This is the behaviour of a baby who is learning to take command of his own self and to determine his own way of being in his environment. It's going to be messy. Food will be everywhere – in baby's hair, in *your* hair, everywhere!

The feeding routine for this age is the same as that suggested for a baby in his second 100 days – from six months on. However it depends on his sleep routine. When a baby gives up his morning sleep, then he will probably benefit from a small snack mid-morning with a slightly later lunchtime meal. This will extend the time that afternoon snack time happens and his dinner meal will probably not start until about 6 o'clock in the evening. It all depends on his sleeping routine, the family routine and, often, the season. It also depends on what time he starts her day. Mealtimes happen around a baby's sleep times and his family's needs.

A baby who is reaching the end of his first year usually requires the same size meals he had previously plus an extra meal (morning snack). This is because his stomach capacity doesn't keep up the same rate of growth as the rest of his body – his height increases, but this growth begins to happen more in his limbs, particularly in his legs.

Milk (breast or formula) is offered at the end of his meal. His milk requirement at this age is 500 to 600 ml of milk *product* – milk, cheese, yoghurt, custard or milk-based sauces. The milk source is breast or formula. There can be a tendency to give massive amounts of formula that fill a baby so that he does not take a balanced diet of solid foods. A baby who takes more milk than he requires is at risk of developing iron deficiency, as he will tend to continue overfeeding on straight cows' milk that has a minimal iron content, rather than enjoying a well-balanced solid diet.

*Average serves*
*1 cup (250 ml) of milk = 1 tub of yoghurt (200 g) = 1 slice of cheese (35 g)*

There is a tendency these days to allow a baby to take a bottle as a comfort, alone, in his cot. A bottle of milk is a substitute for the breast and is to be given in the same way – with the baby cradled in the arms of a loving person. If a baby is left to feed himself in his cot, he is missing some wonderful loving moments. He also runs the risk of developing 'bottle' dental caries or tooth decay, caused by the milk pooling in the mouth, with the possibility of having to have surgery to fill or remove precious deciduous (first) teeth, a not-so-beautiful smile and the difficulty of developing speech.

It is also unsafe practice with a danger of choking. If an infant is put to bed with a bottle of milk either propped to feed or for the child to feed himself to sleep, then milk can travel into the middle ear via the Eustachian tube and pool there. This can lead to an increased risk of middle ear infections and glue ear with the consequences of hearing impairment and compromised speech development, which delay development of social interactions.

A baby's bottle of formula needs to be prepared with joy and love, and to be taken while being cradled in loving arms so that a baby can learn the beauty of closeness with another human being. It also allows a baby to take just the right amounts of milk for his needs, rather than drinking and drinking just to self-comfort and induce sleep.

The drink for a baby of this age is either breast milk, or formula milk, or water.

Fruit juices can be given after the age of two years, diluted with water and only in a cup. If a baby has juice in a bottle, the chances of tooth decay rises and this causes not only problems in baby teeth but also in the permanent teeth that are growing just beneath the gums. A baby needs fruit because fruit pulp provides fibre for the gut, new mouth sensations and good self-feeding opportunities, which help to develop fine motor skills and a healthy self-esteem.

# The dummy

If a baby of this age is still using the dummy as a comfort, then every time it is popped into his mouth, he needs to be in his bed. A baby usually demands or needs a dummy because he is stressed or tired and bed is the place for him in that moment.

If the bed is the designated place for a baby to have the dummy, he soon learns to wean himself from the need for it. Apart from the fact that the dummy can cause nighttime sleeping problems (see First 100 Days), it also can become a habit that, if not curbed, leads to drooling and to impaired speech development.

If the baby in your care is still dependent on the dummy you need to consider 'why am I doing this?' and 'who am I doing this for?' Is it for you or is it for baby?

Often a soft muslin wrap or favourite toy to hold is a great substitute for the dummy, so, when there is a decision to cut back on dummy availability, provide some other independent comfort. A baby will have great difficulty in weaning from the dummy if he is chronically tired or it is past his bedtime.

# TRANSFORMING MOMENTS

A baby's development in this period is dominated by his determination and will to achieve, to act on his intuition, which is the 'knowing' that transcends the mind. Without language, which at this stage a baby has not developed, there can be no reason or ability for structured action. The action of a baby at this age is purely intuitive. It is 'gut feeling', or instinct, which his unformed mind cannot fathom.

In the third 100 days, from age seven months to about ten and a half months, a baby's vision, near and far, is rapidly improving. The near-vision improvement leads to better fine motor skills, which can be observed in play and in the way that a baby can see and pick up a small amount of fluff from the carpet. The development of the ability to oppose finger to thumb is also part of this achievement.

From about nine months he can follow the action of a rolling ball, and will look for fallen toys, often dropping them himself – particularly from his high chair. Food can often substitute for toys, leftovers often deliberately dropped onto the floor just so he can watch them fall. He is not being naughty, he is learning.

If a toy is hidden from his sight, he will look for it. This development comes with his understanding of 'object permanence' – even though an object or person is out of sight, it does not mean that it does not exist.

At ten months, this baby will respond to his own name, and may even respond to a few other names. He can imitate noises that are repeated for him, particularly animal sounds, and click his tongue and he can babble in long repetitive 'strings' of syllables, such as dad-dad or ababa, and later, mum-mum. This babbling will be to himself while he is playing, but increasingly he will babble to other people. This babble is often accompanied by an ability to point and gesture to indicate needs, such as reaching up his arms when he wants to be picked up and held.

When he is able to crawl, he will take himself into hidden places when he needs to do a poo. It is becoming an innate private affair for him – instinctive human behaviour.

## Growth and physical development

The increased development (particularly in length) of the limbs, brings with it greater skills. Some time in this third 100 days an infant will learn to sit unsupported with a straight back, to crawl or bottom shuffle and to stand and begin to cruise around furniture and, ultimately, to walk.

Learning to pull to standing comes before an ability to lower himself from standing to sitting. This can become quite a challenge for parents because often a baby will pull himself up and then not be able to lower himself back down. He needs help! If this happens in the cot at night it can lead to disturbed sleep for everyone.

Until a baby can lower himself into bed, it can help him to stay put if he is swaddled firmly from the waist down, leaving his arms free. This can be stopped as soon as he has learnt to lower himself from the standing position.

His legs can also get caught between the bars of the cot, and a baby will take a lot longer to work out how to disentangle himself. This can be overcome by weaving a length of muslin sheeting taut through the bars so that his limbs will not make their way between them.

It is normal behaviour for a baby of this age to wake two or three times during the night and to talk to the fairies before putting himself back to sleep. This is often the time when he will pull himself to stand in his cot.

Brain growth continues with further insulation of the nerve connections, which in turn leads to further skills development. Hand dominance can be evident, but it is not permanently differentiated until two years of age, when a toddler will show a fairly permanent preference of right- or left-handedness.

The cortex of the brain (the part of the brain that controls, among other things, the development of speech, our intellectual capacities and our social skills) is the part of the brain that shows the greatest development at this stage. The face and the jaw also begin to show the changes that enable the human to have advanced speech.

When the hands-on manipulation of objects (which at this stage begins to replace exploring with the mouth) is matched by the development of vision and touch, and the early development of cognitive or thinking skills that begin to dominate, the baby's purposeful actions become obvious. The recognition of his name and of the words 'no' and 'bye-bye' also demonstrates the development of cognitive skills.

A baby of around nine months, who has good hearing, is eagerly attentive to everyday sounds, particularly the voice. He will shout to gain attention, wait for a response then shout again. He can imitate an adult making playful and other sounds (for example, smacking of lips, coughing) and even word-like sounds of vowel and tune type. If a baby of this age still has only a few monotonous vocalisations, then his hearing needs to be assessed.

# Cognitive awakening

In the third 100 days a baby learns about achievement and to change his environment. He begins to manipulate simple pleasures such as turning the pages of a book, to compare two objects, to transfer objects from one hand to another. He begins to take charge of his eating. He recognises his family as belonging to him and can interact with others with joy and laughter. He can play simple games – peek-a-boo, and clap-hands. This time can be a time of having joy in his life. It is in this period that an infant's cognitive (thinking) abilities are demonstrated in his first acts of problem solving, such as searching for and finding an object that has been hidden from view.

It is also the time when an infant will take his first independent steps in life – to set off on his own path. At first this is with lots of support with his arms, but his feet are firmly planted on the ground.

# Vision

Newborn babies can see objects at a distance of 6 metres about as well as adults can see objects at a distance of 180 metres. At this stage, a baby sees everything in his 6-metre range with the same level of acuity. In other words, he cannot see objects clearly by altering his focus, but he still explores him blurry world by moving his eyes to view his surrounding environment. The visual system matures rapidly over the first few months of life, until at three months of age he can focus quite well on nearby objects.

Colour vision continues to be more refined as the infant matures through the first six months of age, until he is able to group colours by their hues – different reds, different blues, different greens, etc.

Depth perception is the ability to judge the distance of an object from another object and from one's self. This is how we understand our immediate environment and judge our actions in relation to it. When a new baby starts to reach out for an object, he is demonstrating some ability in depth perception. But it is not until he is able to crawl that this becomes quite obvious, because a crawling baby will generally be reluctant to move beyond a sudden drop, such as a stair.

Movement or motion provides a lot of information about depth, and kinetic (movement) depth cues are the first to which an infant becomes sensitive. The other depth cues are binocular (using both eyes) and pictorial (three-dimensional). Kinetic depth cues develop first. So it can be seen that vision is a precursor for action and this is what a baby in his third 100 days is developing into — a *dynamo* or active, energetic child.

A pleasurable activity with a baby of this age is to share a book with him. Babies love to sit in a loving lap and have a simple colourful book read to them. At the beginning of this 100-day period, his attention span is quite short and he will let you know when he has had enough, but this activity provides him with togetherness with another and introduces him to a world of language and a love of books. He is now old enough to join his local library!

# PARENTING WITH VISION

Manipura is the energy centre that provides us with our 'get up and go'. Parenting a child of this age is very physically demanding; it is also mentally and emotionally demanding, using self-control and setting necessary boundaries, not only for your child but also for yourself. It is a challenging time, because we need to separate our own ego from that of the child's, so that he can continue his growth as an individual. This is part of parental growth – understanding that adults cannot learn our children's lessons for them. Children need to explore, achieve and stumble in life, because in doing so they learn.

There is a fine line in how we *perceive* our own power and in how we use our own power. We need to ask: is my own self-esteem in a healthy state? Am I confident but not overpowering with others and in situations in which I find myself. Am I able to draw on my own resources? Or am I 'mouse' power, forever backing away from the challenges in my own life?

And there is also the matter of *owning* your own power. Are you able to look at a situation or conflict and ask 'What has been *my* role in the creation of this situation?' Or do you give your power away by blaming others?

The first three energy centres – Muludhara, Svadisthana and Manipura – are concerned with our physical nature and the development of the ego and with how comfortable we are with our self and with our uniqueness. When interacting with little babies and children remember that they have only been on their journey for a very short time and do not have the knowledge, the life experiences and the type of wisdom that comes with maturity. Their character is only just beginning to form itself. They haven't yet completed their physical growth.

The experience and growth opportunities of parenting is vast – our ego and self-esteem are challenged daily. We need only to look into the mirror of our self, reflected in the eyes of our child, to recognise the inner parts of our *own* self (or of our own inner child) that need nurturing and transforming.

It is also a very good time to reflect on the parenting that we as individuals received when we were children and to understand and accept that our own parents did the very best for us with the skills and resources they had *at the time*. If we see their parenting of us as flawed, then know there is spirituality in imperfection, because we grow out of the challenges that life has offered us.

The positive growth of solar plexus energy is that of the spiritual warrior. When we are experiencing positive and vital energy we feel we can achieve anything that we set out to do – with determination and confidence. This is how we can create change through having a vision and inspiring others. We are inspired by leaders such as Martin Luther King and Mahatma Gandhi, who had the courage to see their vision manifest. They had 'fire in the belly' and inspired their followers to have it too. They created movements that inspired social change. The spiritual warrior draws on the inner strength that is gained from divine force. With this, external challenges are faced and overcome.

When we lack this kind of drive, and have low self-esteem we become dependent on the recognition and approval of others. There is an inner belief of being 'not good enough'. This is known as being a servant or a drudge, a person who is never recognised for a job well done. It is part of having low self-esteem, of having little belief in one's own worth. If 'the servant' begins to believe in his own 'self' and his inner abilities, then others can see them too. Self-acceptance and recognition attracts the recognition and esteem of others.

Every parent wants to be a 'good' parent and our paramount wish for our child is that she be happy. No matter the age of a child, when he is unhappy, the heartache that his parent feels is profound.

*The ultimate measure of a man is not where he stands in moments of comfort and convenience, but where he stands at times of challenge and controversy.*

MARTIN LUTHER KING

# THE FOURTH
# 100 DAYS

# ANAHATA
## *The Heart Chakra*

1. INTRODUCTION

2. ANAHATA – UNCONDITIONAL LOVE

3. THE BEHAVIOUR OF A LOVING CHILD
Tired signs
Crying
Sleeping
Feeding
Inspiring moments

4. PARENTING WITH UNCONDITIONAL LOVE

# INTRODUCTION

The fourth 100 days of a child's life marks the end of babyhood.

The first three levels of consciousness are concerned with our most basic human needs.

Anahata is the bridge spanning the human emotional needs of the basic centres of life and the rational mind, represented by the three higher energy centres. The heart is where the integration of body and mind is achieved through unconditional love.

This is the centre for the *sharing* of love and the beginning of development of compassion for all others. This is where we can love our *self* and, at the same time, we can love others unconditionally.

When a baby is newborn, her heart centre is open and vulnerable, and it is not until the birthing process is completed, during her first 40 days, that her innate need to *physically* protect her heart centre begins to lessen. After 40 days her brain begins to function in those areas that learn to protect her heart in other ways – emotionally and mentally.

If a baby grows up without loving touch and close human contact (as has been observed in orphanages in eastern Europe) she fails to thrive in all areas of her life and her growth. She begins to withdraw emotionally, and she is unable to reach her full potential. In western societies, where our rational mind is regarded as the supreme consciousness and our way of *feeling* is undervalued, we exist in a culture that is dominated by the head. This is why a baby in her fourth 100 days, when she has not yet learnt to rationalise her thoughts, is so generous with her love.

We can learn much about loving from our children.

# The Fourth Energy Centre

ANAHATA
'Unstruck'

## *The Lotus of Twelve Petals*

The Fourth 100 Days
Unconditional Love

COLOUR: Green, the colour of harmony and new growth. It blends the radiating yellow of the third energy centre and the receptive blue of the fifth energy centre. Anahata is also associated with the colour pink, which is the colour of unconditional love.

MUSIC: Choral music, uplifting music that speaks and drifts to our soul, bringing balance to our life. Choral music is devotional music, performed in harmony by amassed voices for the glory of God. The music is generally contemplative and speaks of a love of all creatures.

SENSE: Touch. Of all the senses, touch is the most intimate connection between two individuals.

PHYSICAL BODY SYSTEM: The heart and lungs

ENDOCRINE GLAND: The thymus gland

ANIMAL TOTEM: The Gazelle, a medium-sized antelope. The word gazelle comes from an Arabic word meaning 'to be affectionate' and in Islamic symbolism it represents spiritual states. In the Jewish faith the gazelle symbolises the love for God.

# ANAHATA – UNCONDITIONAL LOVE

Anahata is the energy centre situated in the region of the heart and it stirs in the fourth 100 day period of a baby's life – about ten and a half months to 14 months of age, spanning the time of a baby's transition from her first year of infancy to being a toddler.

This chakra is concerned with the unconditional love that transcends earthly love. It is the kind of love that comes with a *way of being* rather than the love of 'having' or possession. It is the love that comes when we are at one with our own self and with all others. When we experience this kind of love we are in a state of grace, which is a state of acceptance.

Unconditional love means to accept others for who and how they are. There is no judgement. There are no conditions. Anahata's about coming from a space where we can let go of our personal pain or grievances and forgive others for any wrong we feel they may have done. Its lotus symbol has 12 petals representing the first 12 months of life, and the sacramental association of this energy centre is marriage, which is intimate union.

The element of the heart centre is air. Air gives us life, and it gives us the oxygen that the body craves for in every one of its cells. The act of breathing in is known as inhalation or inspiration. The word 'inspiration' is derived from the Latin *in spirito*, to 'draw in spirit': inspiration is not only inhaling air, it is also the body's need to be filled with – or to be in touch with – universal spirit.

Our breath is our primary source of energy for the body, and it is our prime connection with the *life force* or chi from whence our energy comes. The way that we breathe affects the amount of energy that we have, the ways in which we use energy and our general sense of aliveness. When we do not breathe adequately, we are not energised and so we feel depressed and dispirited.

Inhalation, *in halo*, is the only way that our energetic body, our aura, remains integrated with our physical body.

Anahata means 'unstruck'. It is the sound of one hand clapping. It is the sound that happens in the moment of our inspiration. It is the sound of love. It is poetry without sound and poetry comes from the heart.

The sense of the heart is touch. Of all the senses, touch is the most intimate connection between two individuals. Touch is the first of the human senses to develop and it provides us with some of our most essential functions. Touch provides us with a sense of belonging; touch comforts and grounds us. Touch is also one of our most instinctive needs – not only as the desire to be touched but also the desire to touch. We touch each other for many reasons – to show love, to offer comfort and security, but also to help us 'feel' better. As a species, we cannot exist without living physical contact.

When a human embryo is developing in the womb, its heart begins to beat on its 22nd day. On its 26th day, the arm buds appear, and the head begins to fold forward towards what will become its chest. As this happens, the heart moves deep into the chest where it continues to beat, develop and circulate blood. On the embryo's 33rd day, tiny hands appear. As the arms bend at the elbows and tiny fingers appear, the hands grow towards the heart, which they appear to embrace. It is only 40 days after conception – how early we learn to honour and protect our heart and, with our hands, to give loving touch.

Physically the heart centre relates to the heart and lungs. The endocrine gland associated with it is the thymus gland, a small gland situated in the chest in front of the heart, behind the sternum or breastplate and between the lungs.

The thymus gland is the central control organ for the body's immune system. When it is functioning properly, the thymus gland acts like a thermostat to provide the right balance of immunity. It turns up its activity to help the body fight infection or tumour growth, and it turns down its activity in order to prevent autoimmune disease, which is the body's way of fighting itself.

The thymus is relatively large in infancy and childhood, but it begins to grow smaller at puberty and to be almost non-functioning in later life when there is a weakening of the immune system and a susceptibility to disease. The thymus gland releases a hormone called thymosin into the blood stream to assist the white blood cells, lymphocytes in the production of T-cells, which play a very important part in our immune system. The thymus gland is the gland that controls our protective, lymphatic system.

The thymus gland responds to our emotions. When we are happy and are expressing love in our life, it functions well, secreting hormones that tone the heart and keep the lungs active. When we are stressed, the thymus becomes under-active and this is often the time when we seem to be 'run down' and our body expresses this in illnesses and infections.

Emotionally, the heart energy centre is the centre of love, and this love is not only for all others but also for our own self. It does not refer to the love that is associated with material possession or sexual love, because these are based on *need* associated with the first three energy centres.

When our heart energy centre is in balance, we are able to open ourselves to the world and all its creatures and to feel safe with this. When we are 'in love' with life we are balanced and able to express our joy and to share it.

When we have fear, we are unable to breathe fully, our chest contracts and we shut down emotionally. When we experience envy, we are said to be 'green with envy'. Green is the colour of the heart chakra, which implies that we are misdirecting our loving energy from others to ourselves, closing down our heart centre and its capacity to love others, and instead wasting our passion on greed.

Mentally, the heart centre is at the centre of harmony in our life. When we are able to accept our self and accept others for all the frailties that are part of being human, then our mind can be balanced and at peace. When we shut our self off from the world and others, we begin to eat away at our very core. When we love and accept ourselves for exactly who we are in this time and space, then we can do that for others. This is altruism.

When our life can be a daily act of love we have inspiration and purpose.

*It is only with the heart that one can see clearly,*
*for what is essential is hidden from the eyes.*

ANTOINE DE SAINT EXUPERY *THE LITTLE PRINCE*

# THE BEHAVIOUR
# OF A LOVING CHILD

## 'I LOVE'

Anahata, the heart centre, is the energetic core of a baby's ability to love unconditionally. Unconditional love is the love we have when we can forgive ourselves and others for the bruises and bumps that are part of our life experiences and growth. It is the love that comes with acceptance of our self and of others just as we are.

A baby of this age still cannot tell the time or judge distance. Life for this little person is not linear. Life is just now, this very moment: it's me, it's Mummy, it's Daddy, it's Grandma walking through the door, it's the puppy barking. Life is this toy in my hand, or it's my bed. There is no *future* time and there is no *past* time. It's just *now*. All the time is just 'now'.

This does not mean that this baby does not have memory. It is just that she does not measure it or categorise it. So she does not remember that Mummy dished up soup instead of soufflé for lunch. In fact what is 'lunch'? What is 'dinner'? There is only the feeling – hungry or satisfied, with fun in between – eating, drinking, sleeping and playing and not wanting anymore to eat, thank you!

A baby aged from ten and a half through to 14 months is completing her baby year – the year of 'being' her needs. Her first year is a year of having her needs met, of getting on the move and of the triumph of action. The first year of a baby's life is the stirring of the first three energy centres, which are the physical centres of tremendous developments both physical and emotional. It has been a year of taking in and absorbing life.

Towards the end of her first year she begins to form heart attachments to her family and carers – the attachment beyond 'need'. Once she has formed these attachments, then she is able to move out and give of herself instead of internalising herself. She begins to form relationships with other babies.

Here is a baby who has only been on earth for a year. She is learning daily. She is still a human bundle of love, tiredness, crying, sleeping, feeding and growing.

# TIRED SIGNS

When a baby of this age is well fed and she grizzles, then she is tired or sick and needs to be in her bed. Sleep is a great healer and rejuvenator. Tiredness changes from one day to the next. A baby may have a whole week of tiredness when she will need to have 'catch up' sleeps. The next week she may be vibrant and active and not need quite as much sleep.

The weather can have quite an effect on how tired we feel. Windy weather is draining, even if we do not spend much time actually being in the wind. When there is high blustery wind, the electromagnetic energy of the atmosphere intensifies, and consequently we feel a little 'off-centre'. Falling barometric pressure (which happens before a storm) and hot dry seasonal winds create an excess of positive ions in the atmosphere – older people experience respiratory complaints and aching joints, asthma sufferers get tight in the chest, children can become cranky and perverse, and even crime rates rise!

Every time we draw a breath, positive and negative ions fill our lungs and are carried by the blood to our body cells. When there is an increase in positive ions in the air, which happens with dry winds, the body responds with a release of excess serotonin and histamine, which can cause the whole system to be thrown out of balance.

Serotonin is found in many parts of the body – in the brain it acts as a messenger or 'neuro-transmitter'. When there is *too much* serotonin in body cells, we can experience, as well as some physical difficulties, mood changes such as irritability, tension, depression and insomnia. It is all a question of balance.

When a storm breaks, the falling rains bring relief in the form of negative ions, which charge the atmosphere with oxygen, and we begin to notice a change in the way that we feel and an increased sharpness in the way that we think. We enjoy a general feeling of wellbeing. The same happens when we are beside the sea or near a waterfall, where negative ions attach in abundance to the falling water and fine spray. Maybe this is why we sing in the shower and babies love splashing in the bath!

If your baby is irritable and tired consider that she may be affected by the weather. She may need a little more rest time in her bed.

# CRYING

Some time during the fourth 100 days, a baby will begin to cry from the heart. A baby will still yell, but when crying comes from the heart, it comes with a sob – an involuntary sniff as her yelling quietens. As adults cry with a sob this is more the kind of crying that we can understand. But we also know that a 'good cry' can be incredibly releasing and that when it is complete we feel as if we have let go of a burden of sadness. We also let go of anger and this is why we can feel relief. We feel peaceful.

A baby of this age will also begin to cry in protest when she is put to bed. This is often because she would prefer to be asleep before she goes to bed, and it is also because crying is a way for her to unwind so that she can let go of her tension and fall asleep. Often when a baby has finished her 'going to bed' yell, she will pause and start chatting to herself as if some magic happy button has just been pushed. When she has finished his talking, then she will fall asleep. If she doesn't, then it is probably because she has a full nappy. This baby is becoming particular, and she will not sleep with a dirty nappy.

A one-year-old child is fearless and on the move. She has stumbles and knocks and she cries with them, often more from the shock of the event. When this happens, she needs cuddles and comfort. When a baby begins to get overactive and loud, with resulting tumbles, it is often a sign that she is very tired and needs to go to her bed for sleep. If she doesn't have an opportunity for sleep then she will continue to stumble and eventually damage herself.

# SLEEPING

An infant of 12 months has on average 13 to 14 hours of sleep in a 24-hour day. This is broken up into one long sleep overnight of 11 to 12 hours with one or two day sleeps. These times are average times. Some infants can manage very well on a lesser amount of sleep. Some infants need more. Generally a toddler who sleeps well overnight without waking and demanding attention is having enough sleep for her needs. If an infant of this age is unable to sleep through the night without waking for attention, then it could be an indication that she is not receiving sufficient day sleep or that she has not yet learnt to put herself to sleep without an aid and that she needs some kind of parental help every time she wakes.

If a child of this age is still being rocked or nursed to sleep, or is taking a bottle of milk to bed with her, then she has not learnt to put herself to sleep without an aid. The only way to create sleeping through the night is to correct these reasons *during the day* – let her have more sleep during the day and when she does go to her bed she needs to go before she becomes overtired, while she is still awake and without any 'going to sleep' aids.

A baby aged ten months and older will often sleep, then appear to wake, sit up, sometimes utter a yell, then lie down to sleep again. When she does this, she is not consciously awake. She is in a zone of incomplete waking from deep *non-dreaming* sleep. This is known as sleep terrors. Sleep terrors in toddlers are often happening when the child is thrashing around in her bed.

The initial onset of night sleep is followed by a rapid descent into the deepest stage of non-REM sleep. At the end of the first cycle of sleep, which is 60 to 90 minutes, there is a brief arousal to a lighter stage of sleep when the child may even wake briefly. She will fairly rapidly descend into another cycle of deep non-REM sleep. This second sleep cycle of 60 to 90 minutes concludes like the first with a brief arousal to a lighter stage of sleep and maybe a brief waking. The rest of the night sleep alternates between lighter non-REM sleep and longer periods of REM sleep, when there is dreaming.

Then just before morning, a child will often descend once again into a deeper non-REM sleep before waking for the day.

During REM (dream) sleep there is a type of paralysis that prevents moving and the acting out of dreams. It is during non-REM (non-dreaming) sleep that movement is possible, especially during the transitions between the sleep cycles. This is when the infant will sit up or a toddler will have a sleep terror, often immediately at the end of deep sleep. These events happen most frequently during the first four-hour period of evening sleeping. Parents are sometimes unaware that this activity is happening during the early night sleep because this time of the evening is a time of activity for most adults, so there is the 'hum' of industry surrounding them.

The parents who are disturbed by their child's sleep cycles are usually the parents who have allowed their child to stay up beyond a reasonable night sleep onset time.

# FEEDING

An infant of 11 or 12 months can now become a fully-fledged member of the family because she can begin to eat family food. No more boiling and fine mashing of baby foods – this child can now learn to enjoy all the goodies that 'grown-ups' eat, though a strong curry or a plate of oysters may not be an appropriate introduction. Take it slowly – formula can now be replaced with full-cream cows' milk straight from its container. Breastfeeding can continue.

Toddlers often become grazers requiring food in small quantities, but if snacks are wholesome and well balanced then she receives a balanced diet.

Iron-rich foods are important, because iron is required for the healthy development of the nervous system and therefore for her intellectual development.

Milk requirement for children from this age through to adolescence is an average amount of 500 ml per day. This requirement is for milk *product* – cheese, yoghurt and milk in cooking or as a drink*. Cows', goats' and soya milk do not contain sufficient iron, so if a child fills up with large amounts of milk then she is exposed to a risk of iron deficiency and deficiencies of other nutrients that are not contained in milk. These deficiencies lead to imbalance of the whole body, particularly the neurological and immune system. The result is the body's inability to defend itself against infections.

*1 cup (250 ml) milk = 1 tub yoghurt (200 g) = 1 slice cheese (35 g)

## Daily nutritional needs of a toddler

The *recommended* daily nutritional requirements of a toddler are believed to be necessary for balanced development and growth. These recommended requirements are for the average child.

What is regarded as average or normal for one child may not be the average or normal for another. Some children have a big 'appetite' – they have mouths like letterboxes, open all the time for the next offering. Some children eat like birds – a little peck here and a little peck there. Somehow they get to where they are going with their own appetites, and if the food that they do get is nutritionally balanced and the child is thriving, then the quantities are sufficient for them as individuals.

A mother has an investment in what her child eats – and when. So does her child. And it is at this point that a battle of 'wills' can be set up. Once a child can see just how much *power* there is in the process of eating or not eating food, then a pattern of destructive eating over a lifetime can develop.

We live in an age of food fads and we respond to them. We are given the results of the latest findings and warnings around food and we embrace them. However, often this *information* is not balanced. We know that a diet rich in iron is ideal, but we also need to understand that for this iron to be taken up by the body there needs to be an adequate intake of vitamin C and that once in the body, for the iron to be used properly, there needs to be sufficient zinc and even essential fats, which help to bind the iron.

It is all a question of *balance*, not quantities.

If the physical body is well balanced and in a healthy state then we have a good foundation for the balance of our mental, emotional and spiritual states.

Our cultural and social attitudes are also important. Some cultures, such as Italian and Jewish, view food as passion; the French see it as art, and some cultures see food as a means of gathering the clan together. The people of Bali view food as a private affair. They eat when they are hungry, and they eat in silence. They also see food as ritual and festival when wonderful feasts are prepared for religious celebration. When the children in Bali are hungry, they help themselves to available foods that have been previously prepared and stored. There is no set mealtime.

In western societies of *plenty*, our children are suffering from malnutrition, not because of lack of food but because of 'junk food' and bad food choices. There is evidence that some western children as young as ten years, who consume 'poor' diets, are showing early stages of 'furring up' arteries. Teenage girls with high salt and low potassium diets (junk food) are showing early signs of osteoporosis. And this may also be the result of a high phosphorus intake of carbonated drinks that so many children consume.

Toddlers of one to three years of age are grazers. If a child has no real concept of time, then what is the point of set mealtimes? Why have we been raised with the notion that 'if you eat now, you will spoil your dinner'? How absurd is that if your tummy is rumbling with emptiness? And what is the point of having to eat, when your tummy is full, every last crumb of food on a plate because there are children starving in far-away countries?

Where is the balance?

The balance is in the *type* and *variety* of food that is made available for the family. The pattern and the choices start with what you put into your supermarket trolley, the food that you lovingly prepare for your toddler and the eating habits that she learns within her family.

The ideal diet (by food type) for a child needs to consist of:

- 70 per cent vegetables, fruit, grains, beans, pulses and seeds
- 30 per cent fish, meat, dairy products (or vegetarian/vegan equivalents) and added fats.

The World Health Organization recommends that we eat five portions of fruit and vegetables every day.

If you are concerned about your child's nutrient intake, then consider sprouting some beans, pulses, seeds and grains. When *newly* sprouted, they actually increase their nutrient content by more than 200 per cent. Sprouting makes them more digestible, gets rid of the undesirable and bitter qualities of the un-sprouted germ, and it is simple to achieve – just add some non-chlorinated water to some rinsed beans, cover and leave to soak overnight in a warm, dark place! Sprouted beans are also available from the supermarket.

As sprouting beans are a good finger food, toddlers are easily able to pick them up and they usually love their sweet taste. Sprouted germs can be sprinkled onto or crushed into any meals to make the meals more nutritious.

Herbs are also a very good source of essential nutrients. They can be finely chopped and added to your child's favourite meal.

## INSPIRING MOMENTS

At 12 months of age a baby becomes a toddler. Look at how much progress has been made since this tiny, helpless miracle opened her eyes to this world. Her physical growth has been amazing. Typically, an infant increases in length about 30 per cent by age five months and more than 50 per cent by 12 months. Her limbs grow at a faster rate than her trunk, leading to a gradual change in relative proportions. The crown-to-pubis: pubis-to-heel ratio is 1.0: 0.5 at birth. At one year of age this ratio is 1.0: 0.7, indicating a greater growth in length from her hips to her toes.

Her weight proportions change in a similar way. An infant doubles her birth weight by five months of age, and triples her birth weight by 12 months.

Her head growth at 12 months varies due to genetic factors but generally the head and brain has completed half of its postnatal growth and is 75 per cent of its ultimate adult size. This is phenomenal growth!

Her lymphoid tissue, of which the thymus gland is a part, has developed to about 25 per cent of what it will be when she reaches 20 years of age; this will be further discussed when we explore the stirring of her sixth energy centre at about 96 months, or eight years of age.

At birth, a baby's body fat is about 12 per cent of her body weight. Its proportion increases rapidly to 25 per cent at six months of age and then more slowly to 30 per cent at one year. This accounts for her chubby appearance.

Tooth eruption can occasionally happen in the womb but generally teeth start to appear in the fifth month after birth. The occasional baby waits until her first year before cutting her first tooth. By one year of age, the ability to chew is developing well.

When a baby is newly born, her bones are not mature. Bone maturity is a process that continues over childhood. At birth, for example, a baby's wrist is a collection of cartilage. By the time that a baby reaches her first birthday, this cartilage has begun to ossify (a bone hardening or making process) – there are now three separate tiny wrist bones (there are nine separate carpal or wrist bones in the adult). With this development comes a growing ability to move the wrist, thereby enabling the infant to manipulate objects in different ways. She is able to pick up a spoon and put it into her mouth. However, her ability to keep food on the spoon without spilling its contents does not reach any level of competence until she is about 18 months of age. It all depends on her bone development. This is also to be remembered when we are demonstrating or expecting skills of dexterity in a child. Wrist bones continue to differentiate for several years until adolescence.

The bone-strengthening process is also important, particularly with her ability to stand and take steps so that she can begin to cruise around the furniture. Some babies have an earlier ability than others to do this, and if we understand this development we can see that forcing these milestones is not appropriate if the baby's bone development is not adequate.

The ability to reach these milestones of gross motor development often is determined by genetics. If a baby has a parent who was an early walker, then often she will be an early walker. The same applies for 'late walkers'.

At about 12 months of age, an infant sits well on the floor for an indefinite time. She can rise to a sitting position from lying down. She can crawl on her hands and knees, or bum shuffle, and she may even be walking alone. She is able to pull herself to standing and to lower herself down again while holding onto furniture. She 'cruises' around furniture by lifting one foot and stepping sideways. She may stand independently for a few moments. At about 13 or 14 months of age she may be able to crawl up stairs.

Visually she can see clearly at a distance of 3 metres, and can recognise familiar faces from a distance of 6 to 7 metres. She knows where to look for toys that have rolled out of sight and she loves picture books. Outdoor activities are followed with great interest – buses, cars, people, animals and their actions.

Her fine movements are also developing, particularly with her ability to manipulate her toys and to feed herself finger foods.

She can understand simple instructions – 'come to Daddy', 'give to Mummy', 'clap hands', 'wave bye-bye'. She can relate familiar objects to their use, such as taking a brush or comb to her hair.

She knows and responds to her own name and can vocalise most vowels and many consonants.

Her play and social behaviour is a source of wonderment for any observer. This baby loves life. And she loves to express this love. Her attempt to kiss and hug her loved ones is heart melting. To receive one of those big wet kisses is one of life's special moments and a wonderful privilege.

A baby in the fourth 100 days expresses only the positive aspects of love – those that come from the heart.

# PARENTING WITH UNCONDITIONAL LOVE

The English language fails us when we express the word 'love'. How can we equate the way we love our child to the way we love chocolate? But here we have a language that gives us just the one word – love – to express the many meanings of the emotion that we feel.

The ancient language of the Persians had many words for love. There was a word for the love for a camel, a different word for the love of a wife, a different word for the love of a child, a different word for the love of chocolate, and the list goes on.

We, who have the English language, are left wanting. So, what is *love*? And what has love got to do with *life*?

Love is what we feel deep inside us when we feel positive feelings about life or a person or thing that we connect with. Love of nature is a connection that we have for the life of the world that we live in. Love of our home gives us the safety of familiar boundaries that our home provides us with. As human beings, we need to feel safe in our world, no matter how tiny or how vast it is. Love provides us with our guide for survival. Here love has a connection with our first energy centre – our root.

Our love connection is also expressed through our second energy centre when we blossom into the love that comes with passion – the love of sexual desire. This is the love that has enabled the human species to continue to exist.

Our love of achievement and the burning love of our interests – our visions for our world – are manifest through the third energy centre, the solar plexus centre.

But when we get to the love that comes from the heart, we talk about the love that comes when we are able to love others without them having to behave as *we* would like them to.

When we listen to our thoughts and to our words, we can hear when we have love and when we don't. We don't have love when we think of others in a negative way. When we have critical thoughts about others, when we are small-minded and mean and we do things that we are not proud of, then we do not have love.

The great gift we can give our children is for them to see and hear the love within us, and coming from us. We need to be constantly mindful of our thoughts and our words. When we notice critical thoughts, then we need to change them. We can remind ourselves that simply by changing our thoughts we can transform our lives from one of scarcity and meaningless struggle to one of abundance and purpose. At the same time we can ask ourself 'why am I having this critical thought?' Where did this negative thought come from? What am I going to do with it? How can I change this thought? Who am I judging? Is this thought a judgement about myself or is it about another?

When we point a finger at someone else, the other fingers of the hand curl back to point at ourselves.

The only way to protect our heart is to learn to love our own self. The heart is born innocent and pure and in infancy is very open. As we move out into our world – which is part of our family and our culture – the heart is at times wounded, so we begin to wall off those wounded parts in order to protect them. As the wounds accumulate, the walls need to be built higher and stronger to contain them, but in doing this the walls begin to prevent our love that we have to give from getting out. The only way to dismantle these closed-off parts of our heart is with forgiveness – the forgiving of our self for doing wrongs that we think we have done, and the forgiving of others for the wrongs that we believe that they have done.

Out of Mahatma Gandhi's belief in this law of forgiveness and love came the voice of practical non-violence. If we, as parents, are able to work on this within ourselves, then our children can see the possibilities of love and forgiveness and they can learn to forgive and to love themselves. Then they can become compassionate adults able to look *within* themselves for their own healing, instead of searching outside for their healing through developing attachments to other people and to material 'things'.

Forgiveness of another person does not mean condoning their actions, nor does it mean that we have to *like* that person. Forgiveness of another means the letting go of our anger and resentment that we have for that person. When we are able to do this we unburden ourselves and make space within for love. First we need to have a *willingness* to forgive. Until we do, then we remain victims of our situation in relation to that other person and we can get locked into miserable complaining about our circumstances. This does not make us into powerful human beings in charge of our own destiny.

Being loving and compassionate and being able to love our child *unconditionally* begins with loving ourself unconditionally. This can happen when we can accept our own imperfections.

The way to fill and to keep full the well of love within us, and to develop true compassion in our life, is by having fun. When we have fun, we infuse every one of our body cells with positive energy through full breath and its life-giving oxygen. All our body systems function better. In some medical institutions, laughing is used as a therapy.

'Clown doctors' visit sick children to bring fun and happiness to boost their healing processes. The thymus gland, which is the gland of the immune system and which governs the heart energy centre, functions more fully when the heart is light and having fun.

Our mental and emotional health also improves when we are having fun.

If you don't have fun in your life, then find a way to create it – meet with friends, play sport, create a group of like-minded people, have a party or go dancing – and remember to sing.

We live in a world that is so busy working for material gain and honour that it is forgetting to have fun. With this new way of living, children are at the risk of growing up in heartless and uncaring environments. If their environment does not have a passion of the heart and children do not witness charity, how will they be able to respond to the needs of others when they themselves are adults? Children learn by example and they need to see their families, as part of their local communities, helping others in need. The giving of money, while a worthwhile act, is not the *doing* of good deeds. Good deeds require the giving of our time and of our hearts.

When our heart centre is balanced and open, our life is full of love, joy and the fullness of life. It is not influenced by our mind chatter, which has the ability to turn us into an actor whose love is conditional.

The positive, centred heart is the one that is inclusive. The energy that it holds is shared *with* everyone. It generates goodness, it is embracing and it is kind and it has the ability to unite others within its energy. This is the heart that has the capacity to heal. This healing is not only for our own self but also for our relationships, our work, our beliefs, our learning and our nurturing. This is the heart that knows how to sing. It is the lover within. The learning of the heart is to maintain this feeling as a way of life.

Children need the security of seeing their parents and loved ones having fun and fellowship in their lives, and this provides a template for them when they reach adulthood. Memories of the happy, fun times of childhood are the ones that burn brightest and linger longest.

## *My heart a pasture for gazelles*

LBN AL-ARABI
13TH-CENTURY ANDALUSIAN SUFI MASTER AND POET

# SECTION II
# Self-control

# THE FIFTH
# 100 DAYS

# VISUDDHA
## *The Throat Chakra*

1. INTRODUCTION

2. VISUDDHA – COMMUNICATION

3. THE BEHAVIOUR OF A COMMUNICATING, CREATIVE CHILD
Conceptualising
Sleeping
Feeding
Creative moments

4. PARENTING WITH COMMUNICATION
AND CREATIVITY

# INTRODUCTION

The fifth 100-day period marks the end of infancy at 18 months of age and the beginning of the wonderful life of a two-year-old child, which spans from 14 months of age through to three years. It is the threshold of the doorway to higher levels of consciousness and can be a challenging time for both the child and the parent.

For the next six to seven years, this little child will develop basic conceptual skills in preparation for the understanding of abstract concepts that come with higher learning, which is in the realm of the higher energy centres.

A child learns to articulate or utter distinct syllables or words in order to convey feelings, thoughts, desires and distress. But as he is just learning there is bound to be some frustration and mistakes along the way. Throughout life, when we cannot make ourselves understood, our frustration is able to take us into the depths of our rage. This can be a scary place to be.

This is the life of a two-year-old child, who is trying to map out his independence. It is a learning time and a creative time and out of this a child begins to use his negotiating skills and to set and push boundaries with words.

The words on this page are two-dimensional and self-defining – they have edges and spaces and they are symbols for communication. Words enable us to express all the feelings that arise in the lower energy centres and to articulate the thoughts and ideas that come to us through our higher centres. Through these written words, I am able to share my ideas with you, you are able to access them and they set up a line of communication between us. If you are physically with me, then I can speak my words and you can hear them and, in reply, give me yours, and in that way we can establish a bond of friendship and respect and we are able to learn from each other in a three-dimensional world.

Language is the faculty that sets us apart from our ape cousins. Humans have been blessed with the physical structures for speech – the voice box is situated deep in the throat at the epiglottis, which is the valve at the junction of the trachea (windpipe) and oesophagus (food pipe). By 18 months of age, a child's cognitive skills, or processes of *knowing*, are developing and his perceptual capacities and the frustrations that come through the process of learning can be very transparent. This period is a very important time for a little child. *Through* language he develops his creativity and *with* language he can clarify his thoughts.

From about 11 to 14 months, through the growing development of attentiveness, an infant can utter his first few words, generally nouns. A baby may utter first words as early as eight months of age. As his attentiveness through hearing and listening develops further, so does his vocabulary until at 18 months of age, at the end of this fifth 100-day period, he will have 20 to 100 words – and one simple little word, 'NO', is unmistakable. This word, and all the energy that comes with it, is where the challenge lies, but out of this challenge can emerge, if we allow it, an amazing creativity. Little children do not hold back their self-expression. They are totally up-front and speak their truth.

Let hearts, minds and voices sing!

# The Fifth Energy Centre

VISHUDDHA

'Purification'

## *The Lotus of Sixteen Petals*

### The Fifth 100 Days
### Communication, self-expression and Creativity

COLOUR: Blue, the hues of blue that colour the day sky, from pale blue to rich turquoise. Blue is the spirit of truth, peace, contemplation, prudence and fidelity. Blue is a calming colour.

MUSIC: Opera, the most emotional and dramatic of all musical forms. Opera enables us to soar and to weep because it gives us the opportunity to feel and recognise our own unexpressed and unspoken emotions. It reveals to us our own truth.

SENSE: Hearing. It is through our hearing that we develop speech and language providing the means for our communication and self-expression. This is why the association of this chakra is confession, which offers us the way for us to expose our truth so that we can be more truly who we really are. It is known that sound and hearing can have a profound effect on the body's ability to heal and settle itself. The vibrations of sound affect and create physical form. (See Appendix 1.)

PHYSICAL BODY SYSTEM: Ears, throat, mouth, teeth and jaws

ENDOCRINE GLAND: Thyroid and parathyroid glands

ANIMAL TOTEM: The white elephant and the bull. The white elephant represents the law and fertility and growth. The bull denotes strength and fertility and is the symbol of creation, as demonstrated in the Herculean myth of the Cretan bull.

# VISUDDHA – COMMUNICATION

Visuddha, the fifth of the main seven chakras, is the energy centre situated in the neck and it stirs in the fifth 100-day period of a child's life, from the 14th month through to 17 or 18 months of age. Visuddha is the bridge that joins our physical consciousness with our mental consciousness.

Visuddha is symbolised by a lotus of 16 petals and marks the beginning of behavioural development of a two-year old child. This is the period when this energy centre begins to express itself through language, although it comes into its peak power by the age of 30 to 40 years.

The fifth chakra is the gateway to higher realms of spirituality and learning and, in esoteric teachings, it is known as 'the mouth of God'.

Because it is situated in the neck, which joins our head to our body, it is very vulnerable to everything that passes through it – all that we take into our body, through our breath and through what we swallow. It is the centre that helps us determine whether to make decisions of the head or of the heart.

This energy centre is concerned with our self-expression, and with our communion with everything beyond our self. Through our expression we can be creative and through our communication we can purify our thoughts and our deeds.

When it is not functioning openly, we are stuck in perfectionism, we have an inability to express our emotions and our creativity is not flowing.

It is the throat chakra which enables us to develop the ways to give, and also to receive, the gifts of life. One word can change the direction of our life. This is very powerful. Whether we hear it or say it or read it, a single word can determine our history.

Physically, Visuddha, situated in front of the cervical spine and in the inner and outer throat area, involves the throat, the larynx (voice box), mouth, teeth, jaw and ears – all the parts of us that make speech, singing and hearing possible. It is also the part of us that takes in our nourishment and prepares it for digestion, absorption and growth.

The endocrine glands of this centre are the thyroid and parathyroid, which are situated just below the voice box. The thyroid gland controls our basal metabolism and therefore has an influence on body and brain growth and development. The parathyroid gland controls blood calcium and phosphate levels so that nerve and muscle action is smooth and controlled.

The thyroid gland is the first endocrine gland to appear in the embryo. It begins to develop on the 24th day after fertilisation, just two days after the heart begins to beat. Initially it develops below the middle tongue bud, a small swelling on the floor of the developing pharynx (throat), which eventually forms the tongue. At this stage of embryonic development, the thyroid gland is part of the tongue until it begins to descend, as it forms its butterfly shape, to its final location immediately in front of the trachea or windpipe. By the seventh week of embryological development, the thyroid gland has usually reached its final place in the lower part of the neck.

The hormone thyroxine is present in the thyroid gland from the 11th week, just as the embryo is becoming a foetus. It begins to be secreted at about the 17th week after conception and is essential in the foetus and very young child for protein synthesis in the brain and the proper development of nerve cells. If thyroxine is deficient in the foetus then mental development can be affected. After birth, lack of sufficient thyroxine leads to slow physical growth.

Emotionally, Visuddha gives voice to our feelings. Being able to communicate our feelings openly is essential for our life development and we need to feel safe in doing this. If we are afraid to say what is on our mind then we close down, and our throat feels tight and constricted.

Mentally, Visuddha is controlled by the mind and is its voice. It allows our inner reflection, our inner dialogue. When this energy centre is true and balanced, then our outer communication is clear and graceful. It is also the source of silence, which often can speak louder than words. Knowing when and how to communicate is its strength. When we have a quiet and open mind then we are able to listen to our own intuition.

This centre is the key to our individuality through expressing our truth.

The element of this centre is ether. The ether is an invisible elastic 'substance' that is believed to be distributed throughout all space. It is the ether that supports or contains the particles that make up our world – the air particles – and matter. Ether is the essence of us. It is the part of us that renders, or translates, the spiritual part of us that we call our 'essence'. Our life story, or history, tells of our existence, but it is the *essence* of us that reveals our own extraordinary unique nature.

The quintessence, (from the Latin *quinta essentia*, meaning fifth essence) is the purest concentrated essence or element of anything or anyone. It is the element of truth – essence is what makes a thing what it is. It is what is *essential* for defining its existence. It is also the unique quality that is assigned to the individual.

Our essence is contained in the ethereal part of us, within our ether that extends from within and out beyond our physical body to be part of the ether that surrounds the planet. It is through the ether that we are able to connect our energy with the energy of others. On a platonic level, it is through the 'ether' that we are able to communicate electronically, through the *ether*net or, as we know it, the 'internet'.

Visuddha means 'purification'. It is through purification that the body regenerates itself. Cells are constantly cleansing themselves with oxygen and nutrients, and when they have outgrown themselves they are replaced with new and fresh ones. The body is in a constant state of renewal in its efforts to maintain homeostasis – the state of balance and health. The mental and emotional and spiritual parts of us are also in the same motion, striving to be pure and to continue growing and evolving. If one part of us becomes stagnant, then the other parts of us are thrown out of balance. We live in a continuous rhythm of cycles – night followed by day, the moon cycles, the tides, the seasons – to which we respond internally with our own cycles – sleeping, waking, menstruating, hibernating. Visuddha is the rhythm and hum of life.

Visuddha is also represented by the symbol of the bull, a strong, determined animal symbolic of creation and fertility.

But the bull can also represent stubbornness and uncontrolled creation ending in chaos. In Greek mythology, the hero Hercules' seventh labour was to capture the wild, ravaging, fire-breathing Cretan bull and take it back alive to Greece. The bull was originally to be a sacrifice to the god Poseidon, but was kept by King Minos, who was too impressed by its strength and beauty to sacrifice it, even though it caused nothing but destruction and chaos throughout his land. Hercules had to use sheer strength to immobilise the bull, literally taking it by its horns. He then carried the subdued Cretan bull back to Greece on his shoulders, draped around his neck.

This legend tells us that in order to grasp a new opportunity, we need to let go of, or sacrifice, some old ways or possessions, no matter how impressive, that are no longer appropriate for this new way. The bull is our creative energy, which can become a destructive, uncontrollable force, but it can also be great creative potential through the healthy development of this energy centre.

Through the fifth energy centre we can harness our will, we can be true to our self and we can live creatively.

# THE BEHAVIOUR OF A COMMUNICATING, CREATIVE CHILD
## 'I SPEAK'

*In the beginning was the Word, and the Word was with God and the Word was God.*

So says John 1: 1 to describe how the creation of the Universe came about through the vibration of sound. We are articulate beings and with every sound that we utter, just as matter is created by sound, we create our life reality. Language, through words, is communication in a distinctly human manner. It is the grouping of symbols to convey meaning on a two-dimensional plane. It is through *spoken* language that we are able to exist in a third dimension.

As a small child develops language skills, he begins to exist in a three-dimensional world, where his life has layers and meanings and concepts and where his life extends beyond the two-dimensional world of fundamental life.

From birth he begins to relate the different senses to each other. What he is able to see can have an association with how it might feel or it might taste. It is about learning the concept of cause and effect and the inter-relationship of all things. Now he begins to bring all that learning into a form of communication through language.

Language develops rapidly over the early childhood years. It is the speed with which children gain a vast vocabulary and an intricate grammatical system that demonstrates the rapid growth of a small child's cognitive abilities.

The acquisition of language is one of the most amazing and necessary achievements in life. It allows for phenomenal learning, it enables social development and interaction, and it provides a child with the opportunity to reach his full potential and ultimately his true purpose in life. If a baby is hearing impaired then this achievement is a much greater challenge, though certainly far from impossible. Helen Keller, who through serious illness as a very small child, lost her sight, her hearing and her capacity for speech, managed to find a number of ways to communicate and connect to the people around her even without the use of these senses. Her story, among others, shows that the fifth chakra can vibrate and create the interaction we need as human beings even if its most common instruments are impaired or incapacitated.

The development of language is further described in Appendix II.

## CONCEPTUALISING

Conceptualising is the process of conceiving a general notion or idea. It requires cognition and the ability to apply or carry out the idea in a practical and meaningful way. Conceptualising is the ability to *think through* an idea or image.

Cognition is the act or process of awareness and the acquisition of knowledge. The word 'cognition' comes from the Latin *cognitus*, which means 'to get to know'. Cognition is the result of mental activity – such as remembering, creating, problem solving, symbolising, fantasising and even dreaming. It begins with our ability to have rational thought. Cognition develops as a child begins to interact with his world and the people in it. It is difficult to determine how the acquisition, or understanding, of language can potentiate our cognition.

When a term baby is in his first month of life, his existence is responsive: he is a little bundle of reflexes that are physical responses to his environment. From about one to four months of age, his simple movements are orientated toward his own body. He begins to watch his own hands, he responds to pleasure with a smile, and he begins, towards the fourth month, to make more purposeful movements, such as reaching his hands out to an object such as a toy.

From four to eight months, the second 100-day period, a baby learns to repeat behaviour to recreate effect, and he also begins to imitate familiar behaviours such as laughing and noises like blowing a 'raspberry'. From there until he is about 12 months old, his actions become much more intentional – he develops an improved anticipation of events, such as making a musical toy work, and he can realise that a toy that has been hidden is still in existence (object permanence).

When a baby enters his second year, he begins to develop ways of 'experimenting' with objects in new ways – she begins to place blocks one on top of the other, or he might begin to 'use' a hairbrush by pushing it across his head. He will look for a hidden object in more than one place. He begins to understand and respond appropriately to a simple spoken instruction or suggestion – 'let us find your coat', 'where are your shoes?', 'can you find your book and we'll have a story'.

From about 18 months of age until he is about two years old, a child begins to demonstrate that he is processing his thoughts. He begins to problem solve. If an object is stuck, he will manipulate it from many angles in order to free it rather than pull at it from one position – where he is. He begins to see other possibilities.

He also begins to imitate the actions of other people, even if they are not present. He may be playing and will be seen doing something that he had seen his father do a few days ago. He is drawing on the memory of what *someone else* has done rather than a memory of what he himself has done previously.

The behavioural development of a child to the age of two years was observed and described by the child psychologist Jean Piaget as the sensorimotor stage of cognitive development.

It is difficult to comprehend the development of cognition without a little understanding of how the human brain and its parts grow and develop throughout infancy and childhood. This growth and development happens in stages according to a well-organised plan.

# Brain development

The brain is like a garden. There are periods of planting, of great growth, of pruning, moving and of dying off. Firstly, it is all planted out in an amazing design. This starts in the embryo, during the first ten weeks after conception.

The growth continues throughout the foetal stage and then from birth throughout life. Like plants in a garden, which grow at different rates according to their species, different parts of the brain grow and develop (or specialise) at different rates.

Today, there is more knowledge of the *structures* of the brain than there is about *how* this amazing and complex organ works. The rate at which the *size* of the brain accelerates peaks in the foetus at about 30 weeks after conception. Its growth *rate* thereafter declines. However the rate of growth of the brain in the first two years after birth is still phenomenal. At birth, the brain of a full-term baby averages about 25 per cent of an adult brain; at six months it weighs nearly 50 per cent; at two years it is about 75 per cent of its adult weight. When a child is five years old, his brain will weigh 90 per cent of its adult size and at ten years of age, the brain will be 95 per cent of its adult weight. When these weights are contrasted with the weight of the whole body, which at birth is about 5 per cent of the young adult weight, and at ten years about 50 per cent, it can be seen that compared with the rest of the body, the growth and development of the brain is amazingly rapid. The development of a child's cognitive skills, the process of gaining knowledge and abilities match this brain growth.

The brain has three main divisions: the forebrain, the midbrain, and the hindbrain. The brain is joined to the spinal cord by the brain stem. The brain of a newborn term baby weighs about 400 grams. It is fairly well developed in the part of the brain stem called the medulla oblongata, which is continuous with the upper part of the spinal cord, and also in the midbrain, which lies just above the base of the skull. These are the areas of the brain that regulate the vital functions for the sustaining of life – such as our heartbeat, our breathing, and our blood pressure. Also controlled in the brain stem are the actions of swallowing, coughing, vomiting, sneezing and hiccuping — all of which little babies are fairly good at doing.

The midbrain influences our pleasure sensations, our mood, our sense of reality and our motor (movement) function. It has generous connections with the cerebral cortex and with the limbic system, during and after they have completed their process of myelination or insulation of nerve connections.

At birth, the newborn brain has a fairly full complement of cells — neurons and glial cells (neuroglia). Neurons are the brain cells that store and send information. The neurons are supported by the glial cells, which form a protective coating and nourishment for the neurons. Glial cells are essential for providing structural support for the growing and developing neurons and they continue to multiply throughout life.

After birth, growth and development of the brain involves the creation of synapses, or connections between the neurons. This process, occurs so rapidly in the cerebral cortex during the first two years after birth that it contributes to the threefold increase in the weight of the brain in that time.

The cerebral cortex, or grey matter, particularly that of the forebrain, seems to be the centre of the intellect. It has some control over our emotions and our instincts. It also has higher control of more advanced motor or movement function, memory, perception, visual processes and speech. The frontal lobes of the forebrain are involved in movement, complex judgment, emotional regulation, problem solving, decisions, planning and creativity.

For two years after birth, two clear gradients of development occur. The first gradient is concerned with the order in which general functional areas of the brain develop. The first functional area to develop is the motor (movement) area. The next area to develop is the sensory area where the nerve fibres that enable the sensation of *touch* end. The primary visual area in the occipital lobe where nerve paths from the retina in the eyeball end follows this area. Then follows the primary hearing area in the temporal lobe.

The second gradient is concerned with the order in which bodily localisations advance within the areas. Within the motor and sensory areas, the order of development within each area is firstly the mouth, followed by the tongue, lips, hands, arms and finally the legs. The first meaningful smile that a baby gives is amazing, not only for the sheer beauty and wonder of it, but also because it is an indication that the part of the motor area that has begun to develop concerns the muscles surrounding the lips. Up until now, the part of the cortex of the brain that has been developing in the motor area has been the area concerned with the strong coordination of sucking – the mouth and tongue. This is for a good reason. A baby must firstly be able to efficiently take in nourishment for his survival. His next need is his interaction and engaging of others to ensure this continued nurturance. He does this with a smile, and it is a winner.

Brain development is not always smooth and continuous. During the first year, there is a rapid growth of nerve connections. A 'pruning' of connections in each area of the brain then follows this, as the wiring of the brain becomes more efficient and any redundant pathways and connections are eliminated. The pruning of pathways that takes place at about 18 months of age is believed to be a response to the child's experiences of life so far. The pathways that are left in place are the most efficient pathways. Because there are always new experiences in life, new pathways are always being formed and ones that are not used are being deleted. This is a lifelong process as we continue to learn new skills. Pruning does not take place in all areas of the brain at the same time. In the area of the brain that has to do with language comprehension and production, connections do not achieve their maximum density until a child is about three years of age. It is after this that pruning begins in this area. It is not until a child is four years old that the beginning of pruning is happening in all areas of the brain. Pruning continues in spurts throughout childhood, adolescence and into adulthood.

The brain has a remarkable ability to reorganise itself into optimal efficiency. This is called *brain plasticity*. It is also the way that the brain can reorganise itself following injury. It is recognised that the brain needs sufficient stimulation for this organisation to take place, and as the brain has a peak time of plasticity during early childhood, then it becomes obvious why a small child spends so much active time exploring his environment and has an insatiable appetite for learning. If this stimulation of learning and discovery is missing in the early period of brain growth and plasticity of a child's life, then the brain does not reach its full potential. There are other growth spurts into early adulthood and throughout life, new connections are forming, myelination or insulation of these connections is occurring, and old connections are dying off. There is also fresh evidence that new neurons are produced in the brain throughout life.

The limbic system in the brain is situated deep within the lower part of the cerebrum, at the top of and bordering the brain stem, and is regarded as the emotional part of the brain. (The word 'limbic' means border.) It is found in all mammals and is associated with olfaction (smell), memory, autonomic (involuntary) functions of the sympathetic nervous system and certain aspects of emotion and behaviour. It is the area of the brain most involved in experiencing and expressing emotions and the core processing area for the human emotions of fear, rage and pleasure. It focuses on self-preservation, reproduction and the formation of memories.

Even though the limbic system is quite well developed at birth, there are some functions that are still quite immature in a small child of two years. It is good to keep this in mind when we begin to have high expectations of the emotional behaviour of a small child. All *emotional* experience results from the activation of the limbic system. An emotion can be triggered in us even without the thinking part of the brain knowing why or what it is. This is particularly true of anxiety and stress, and we all react in different ways to this emotional pressure.

Infants in the first few months of life show differences in how they respond to new situations. Some react with agitated movements of their limbs, arching of the back and fretting and crying episodes, while others show very little response. This all depends on genetic makeup (nature) and the way that their families react to similar situations (nurture). It is now believed that different parts of the brain process different emotions by a system of receptors taking up molecules (neuropeptides) specific to each emotion. These molecules of emotion, released from the limbic system, circulate in the brain and through the body in much the same way as hormones do, which suggests that the brain itself is one big endocrine gland.

It is known that the prefrontal cortex, or thinking part of the brain, can deal with our emotions in different ways, depending on its maturity. It is through this knowledge that methods of biofeedback therapy are designed; how and why different types of counselling are used, and how self-regulation can become a way of life. Our elders believed that 'by having good thoughts our worries would cease' and there is some merit in this.

Because the processing or thinking part of the brain (the cerebral cortex) is still immature in a small child, it stands to reason that he does not have the capacity to cope well with his emotions. We only have to take a trip to the local supermarket to see this. Whether it is our child or someone else's, we often see 'thoroughly bad behaviour'. This little child wants pleasure, and when he can't have it he has plenty of rage. Reasoning with him is useless – the part of his brain that he needs for this reasoning just isn't properly organised yet, and the emotional and memory functions of the limbic system are still quite immature. This is why *formal* schooling is delayed until a child is five or six years of age.

The hippocampus is a major part of the limbic system and is closely related to the olfactory (smell) processing function of the brain. It is one of the primitive or early developed areas in terms of the evolution of the brain. This area is involved in the emotions and is also important in the processing and storing of *long-term* memories and higher learning.

In a small child this area is still developing, so self-awareness and his ability to maintain routines over a period of time does not gain a degree of maturity until the end of preschool age. The hippocampus (and there are two in the brain) is a major part of the limbic system. These areas of the brain are deeply involved in our emotional lives. They are also involved in the transfer of information to our long-term memory. As this area of the brain matures during the preschool years, memory function improves rapidly. It is also during this time that fears and anxieties can be laid down through memories of unpleasant or frightening life events, such as a negative episode with a dog, being filed away in long-term memory. That is why adult responses to a child's experiences need to be handled with calm reassurance and with understanding, rather than with dismissal. A small child's fright needs to be validated and he needs to know that it is OK to feel scared and that he is not being laughed at or 'being silly'. Gradually he can come to know that this fright can lessen, as he grows bigger.

The cerebral cortex is the area of the brain that has maximum development between the ages of two and six years. The fibres that link the cerebellum, which is the area of the brain associated with movement coordination and memory of movement patterns, to the cerebral cortex do not have their full complement of insulation until a child is about four years of age. This is why little children appear 'clumsy' because they do not have fine control of voluntary movement.

The reticular formation, situated in the most central part of the brain stem and extending downward into the spinal cord, is a part of the brain that is necessary for the kind of alertness that is necessary for survival. Especially developed in humans, it is concerned with the maintenance of attention and consciousness; the nerve connections in this area continue to insulate at least until puberty and beyond. This process is necessary for the development of our 'attention span', which is the length of time that we can maintain our attention or focus on a particular task.

The reticular formation is also an alarm system because it serves as an alerting system, helping the eyes to reflexively track and focus in fight-or-flight situations. Until this area of the brain has reached some level of maturation, there are varying degrees of ability to assess a dangerous situation, such as the hazard of traffic, cliff edges and sharp knives, which explains why it takes a little child a while to grasp the rules and dangers of crossing the road.

The reticular formation also plays a role in our emotional responses to life situations, and because the trigeminal nerve, which controls the mouth, biting and chewing, has many connections here it is probably associated with teeth-grinding (bruxism) or clenching in both children and adults that results if our 'life stress' is not dealt with in other ways.

The temporal lobe of the cerebral cortex contains areas involved in hearing and in understanding speech. It has connections to the hippocampus and amygdala of the limbic system, the important parts of the brain that deal with learning, memory and emotion. The temporal lobe also plays a prominent part in integrating our inner experiences and providing us with our sense of identity.

Situated behind the temporal bones of the skull, just above and behind the ear, the two temporal lobes of the brain are in fact not identical. The upper surface of the temporal lobe is, on average, considerably larger on the left side than on the right, a difference that is established during foetal life. The temporal lobes are chiefly concerned with the analysis of sounds and it is the left lobe which predominates in the activities of receiving, processing and producing language. It is in the left hemisphere of the brain that nuances of language, such as rhyme, are realised, while in the right hemisphere a word is understood for what it means.

This difference is indicative of a process called brain lateralisation, where the two hemispheres of the brain begin to show dominance in certain areas. This is easier to understand when we consider our right- or left-handed dominance. This dominance is evident in early infancy at about five or six months of age and it is established at about two years of age, both ages coinciding with spurts in language competence. When language is developing rapidly it places a greater burden on the left cerebral hemisphere, which results in a temporary loss in motor dominance that returns as each new language skill stage – first babbling, then first words and finally word combinations – become established.

If the left side of the brain controls the right side of the body and the right side of the brain controls the left side of the body, then we can understand a little more clearly how different parts of the brain control specific parts of our bodies.

The temporal lobes of the brain have growth spurts that peak at one and a half to two years of age and then again from 17 to 20 years of age – and maybe that can help us to understand why teenagers as well as two year olds speak a 'different' language to the rest of us and also why they experience such an incredible journey in establishing their own identity.

Self-conscious emotions first appear at the end of the second year, as the sense of self emerges, and these emotions are also quite acute in adolescence. To get to where we are as adults and how we perceive our *self* (identity and self-consciousness), we can be aware that we have taken the same journey through infancy and adolescence. It is also during these times when the different parts of the brain are going through rapid and intermittent growth and development that positive encouragement and stimulation are essential for the optimal development of the child, not only physically but also mentally, emotionally and spiritually.

The parietal lobes of the brain, situated posterior to the frontal lobes, are involved in sensory reception and interpretation and in the motor or movement parts of speech. The cortex of this area of the brain also receives and interprets information of the outside world that has been received through the different senses of the body. It then is able to determine appropriate responses to this information. For instance, if we see an object flying towards us, it provides the motor information that enables us to move away from and to protect ourselves from the object. It works closely with the areas of speech that are situated in the temporal lobe.

The occipital lobes of the cerebrum are situated at the back of the brain. They are involved in the receiving, interpreting and relaying of information that comes through the sense of sight. This is where all the wonderful information that is provided by our faculty of vision, such as the light, colours and forms of our world, is brought to our consciousness. The nerve fibres of the optic or sight-receiving system begin the process of myelination or insulation just before birth with the main burst of growth between 30 and 34 weeks after conception (week 28 to week 32 of pregnancy).

After birth, the process is completed fairly rapidly, with visual ability rapidly developing dominance over the other senses. We are, most of all, visual creatures, and we rely on our sight to learn more of this world than is possible through the other senses. Sight is essentially the *sense of survival*, for without sight, humans would not be able to hunt for or gather their food.

The cerebral cortex, or grey matter, is the thinking and motor part of the brain. It is constructed in six layers. These layers appear to develop first from the inner, deeper layers then outwards to the outer or superficial layer of the brain, much like the layers of an onion. The motor and sensory areas of the cerebral cortex that are situated in this outer layer of the cortex control the lower parts of the body – the lower parts of the torso and the legs.

This is reflected in an infant's motor development – he has less control over these areas than he does over his mouth, tongue, lips and his upper limbs. As the process of nerve insulation continues, an infant begins to develop a degree of control over bowel and bladder, and this is evident in more regularity of his bowel action and longer dry spells between nappy changes. It also accompanies greater leg control. An infant stands before he can walk, often within his first year, but he is still a fair way off being able to kick a ball with intent. This he will be able to do when he is around two and a half years of age.

When a child starts to do different things with intention, such as grasping an object at about four months after birth, he is beginning to learn how to control his environment. By the time he is 18 months of age, he is intentionally moving about in his environment. Every day he is venturing further and learning his place within the world. While this development is going on he is also developing an ability to *conceptualise* – the ability to work his way through an idea.

The corpus callosum is part of the white matter situated deep in the brain and it connects the two cerebral hemispheres via about 8 million cross-over nerve fibres, which enable the hemispheres to communicate with each other. This part of the brain is present in the foetus from about the third month after conception, but myelination of the corpus callosum does not begin until the end of the first year after birth. Its development is fairly well advanced in a child of four to five years of age, which is when children become more proficient at tasks that require the transfer of information and coordination between both sides of the brain.

Using both sides of the brain enables us to have complex thought when lateralisation (the slight differentiation of the structure and function of the two hemispheres of the brain) is advanced and the corpus callosum has gone through the process of myelination. If the left side of the brain has the dominant centres of language, logic, analysis and maths, and the right side of the brain has the dominant centres of intuition, creativity, art, music and special perception, we can have messages from all these centres passing between the two cerebral hemispheres via the corpus callosum to bring richness to our ideas. All of us, as individuals, have special dominances of the different centres of the brain, but it is within our capacity to develop every area through special exercises, repetition and determination in order to create new ways of thinking and to view things and experiences from 'different angles'. If we don't work our brain as much as we are capable of, then we lose our talents.

An orange is not only food. It is shaped round like a ball, its colour is orange, it smells sweet and it contains juice. It is a fruit that comes from a tree before it comes to the supermarket. This information needs to be processed by both sides of the brain and brought together through a bridge between the two hemispheres of the brain – the connections of the corpus callosum.

A two-year-old child probably won't get much further than the fact that the colour of an orange is *orange* and that its shape is round, but by the time he is four or five years old his description will be much more extensive. It all has to do with the rate of his brain development, the connections between both hemispheres and his communication skills. It also has a lot to do with how much stimulation and input he is receiving throughout his childhood. It is known that a child who is encouraged and helped to learn new skills, who eats a well-balanced diet rich in iron and who lives in a loving and safe environment has enhanced growth of new pathways within the brain.

# Self-control

Self-control is the exertion of our own will on our personal self – in our behaviours, our actions and in our thoughts. Self-control develops from how we see our self, and an ability to set up boundaries for our 'self'. It is an important skill for a child to learn because it allows the child to have power or control over her own actions.

Learning self-control is about a child learning to make choices about his own behaviour. If a child begins to learn self-control at an early age, then he will feel better about the choices that he makes throughout his life.

The development of personal control is a life-long process and it is the ability to make decisions about how and when to express our feelings and which of our impulses on which to act. We begin to learn self-control with the growing development of our cognitive skills and our ability to understand our own self, how we are as individuals and our ability to understand others.

A toddler, who literally is only just beginning to master walking and standing on his own two feet, has a fairly long way to go, because if we look at our language we see that 'understanding' is the act of one who understands. This is a mental activity and yet it is under-standing – being firmly grounded with 'both feet on the ground'. In the beginning, for a toddler, there is a lot of staggering and lurching, stumbling and falling. Understanding is not knowledge. Knowledge is something that we gain from outside of our self, whereas understanding is something that we gain from within our self. Understanding is unique and belongs purely to the individual. Knowledge exists for all people to share.

*Under*-standing is a great metaphor for having self-control. The abilities of standing, walking, running, climbing stairs, kicking a ball, skipping, balancing on one leg and dancing do not come all at once – they are achieved over a fairly lengthy period in the life of a small child. Throughout life, understanding is a gradual process and it happens when a light goes on within us. And for this to happen we need to be earthed or well grounded.

# Toileting

One of the first acts of physical self-control that we are asked to perform as a child is toilet 'training', requiring control of the deep muscles of our body, particularly the pelvic floor. Voluntary control over these muscles only begins to develop at about 18 months of age, at about the same time as a child's growing ability to conceptualise becomes evident.

Healthy self-control involves sensitivity to feedback and a willingness to be flexible, creative and decisive. Self-control also involves surrender – letting go, trusting our environment and our relationships. So when we embark on the process of toilet 'training', the physical, emotional and intellectual activities that are involved can be a metaphor for the delicate balance of control and surrender that applies to other areas of life. It is also about trusting life processes.

The ability to conceptualise comes with the continuing development of the brain through the ongoing process of myelination of the connections between the nerves and the brain cells and from brain cell to brain cell. As this development is happening in the parts of the brain of a child up to one and a half to two years of age, the child is gradually able to conceive of an idea and be able to work with it by forming it in his mind or to imagine it and then to understand it. He then develops the ability to formulate or express the idea through words and actions. This ability is necessary for the child to begin to learn the process of toileting himself.

Toileting requires readiness on the part of both the child and of the parent. In other words, the time to commence toilet training with a toddler is when you and he are *both* ready.

You, as trainer, are ready when you can see a fairly clear path ahead – that is, you are not about to be stressed out with a house move or the arrival of a new baby or with some other venture that requires a lot of your physical and emotional input. You need to be prepared for not knowing how long the process will take and that you are in good humour, so that you are able to deal with a toddler's sometimes challenging behaviour. The time is right when you feel that you and your child are not in a frustrating or negative stage of your relationship together, and also that you can be prepared to abandon the process if it becomes obvious that it needs a rest before starting it all again. You are ready when you feel that you have tons of patience, which is essential for coping with any ' accidents' and also for remembering that a little child has *no* concept of time management.

You are ready when you *intuitively* feel that 'the time is right'. Listen to your inner voice.

A toddler's readiness for self-toileting generally happens anytime from two to four years of age. Occasionally, a toddler may be ready at about 17 months of age at the end of this fifth 100-day period. If a small child is still not showing any signs of interest in toileting after four years of age, then he needs a medical assessment.

A small child is ready when he can follow simple instructions and understands toileting words such as 'wee', 'poo', or whatever his family words are. He needs to be able to differentiate between 'wet' and dry.

When he has longer 'dry' spells of two hours or more, it is an indication that his nerve connections are maturing and that his pelvic floor muscles are strengthening and beginning to control urine flow. This is a sign of his readiness. Developing a regular pattern of bowel movements is another fairly good sign, though not all toddlers can fulfil this requirement, especially if they have frequent or constipated bowel movements (for which there also needs a medical check-up).

A toddler is also ready when he is showing signs that he wants to do things independently, such as a willingness to help with dressing himself, with simple tasks such as pulling his pants up and down; when he is going through a phase of wanting to please you, and when he appears to be feeling secure and happy.

If there has been a disruption in a small child's routine, such as an illness or moving house or because there is a new baby in the home, then it is a fairly good idea to delay introducing the learning process for at least one to two months.

Delaying the learning process until warm weather days is also best for success. A small child is better able to help himself if he doesn't have to cope with the bulk of cold weather clothing. Going without any clothing at all helps a child to understand cause and effect – that a certain effect goes with the feeling and the action that leads to relief. The whole learning experience then gains a new meaning – the process of conceptualising or thinking his way through the idea.

If a small child begins to balk or resist the process, it is usually due to starting the process too early. He needs to have a rest from it all and then start again. Revise everybody's readiness before restarting the process.

One of the most satisfying aspects about toilet training with a child is that it is a partnership – something that has been achieved together. It is a time when a toddler begins to realise his place in the family and a way to be part of a team. It is a great time for a small child to learn about achievement. If it has all become a struggle or a conflict, then a child will probably not have a very happy outlook on qualities that are associated with formal and life education – persistence, praise, reaching goals and moving onto others, and also the choices that can go hand in hand with those qualities. In the greatest outcome, the child is toilet trained, he has learnt that learning can be fun and that achieving is very satisfying. He also learns that it is OK to make blunders in life and that these can be dealt with, and that there are always opportunities available for trying again and again to succeed with whatever he is undertaking.

# SLEEPING

A newborn baby spends half of his sleep time in REM sleep (rapid eye movement sleep or dream sleep) and half of his sleep time in non-REM sleep (non-rapid eye movement sleep or non-active deep restorative sleep). By the time he is one year old this proportion has changed to about one-third REM sleep and two-thirds non-REM. When he reaches two years of age, he will spend a quarter of his sleep time in REM sleep and three-quarters in non-REM sleep. An adult has about one-fifth of sleep in REM active sleep. So it can be seen that in his second year, a child's sleep pattern is becoming more adult-like.

He will sleep on average, 13½ hours in a 24-hour period, 11½ hours in long night sleep and one to two hours in daytime sleep. Some toddlers resist day sleeping, but sleep extremely well through the night. If this child sleeps soundly through the night without needing help through his sleep cycles, then this is a satisfactory pattern. When a small child is disturbing his family throughout the night, then this needs to be rectified as it leads to very tired and resentful parents and carers, and consequently impacts on family harmony. When this happens, it needs to be determined why this child cannot manage to sleep conforming to his age-group pattern. Professional help is sometimes needed to determine this.

Middle ear infections, urinary tract infections and teething can impact on a child's ability to sleep. Using (or losing) a dummy can also cause a child to disturb his parents. Inadequate clothing, particularly on feet and legs, may cause a disturbance of sleep. Cold feet are very difficult to sleep with, no matter what age we are. A pair of socks or leggings can make a great difference to a baby's ability to sleep soundly.

If an infant has never been a good sleeper, then this can be the result of having not been able to develop a good sleep routine and pattern, and generally this child suffers from chronic tiredness (as do his parents). This sleep pattern becomes a circular problem, which really needs professional intervention. Changing a daytime eating and sleeping routine can turn the nighttime sleep pattern around (see the Second 100 Days section).

Some time in the second year, an infant will drop his second daytime nap. Usually, a child in the second year will switch to one daytime nap and this is usually in the afternoon straight after an early lunchtime meal. There are times when a child is just so irritable, accident prone and grizzly that he needs to sleep even though the timing does not coincide with his usual pattern. He needs a catch-up sleep.

The amount of energy that a small child expends during the day is phenomenal. He just doesn't stop. He doesn't know that he needs to sleep. He doesn't have any concept of time. He is still a child with a bundle of sensations and emotions. He is either a dynamo or he is hungry or he is tired. When a child becomes tired, he becomes very loud. Listen to him, not the clock, and let him have a catch-up nap. He'll probably protest, but he will cope a lot better and sleep better overnight.

Children in their second year can have anxieties about being isolated in a dark room, cut off from the buzz of family life. Imaginative play comes with the development of conceptualising, and this is part of the richness of this fifth 100-day period in a child's development. This imagination can also create all sorts of scary things that go bang in the night. Confining a toddler in his own darkened room can create a situation that is not conducive to his being able to happily settle himself to sleep without a lot of help.

Another reason why a small child finds it difficult and scary to go to bed is the result of nightmares or 'bad' dreams. Dreaming is a means that the psyche uses in order to process life events. As a toddler grows and develops, his experiences expand and lead his into unknown territory. He is now on the move and exploring and also experiencing rapid brain development in the area of conceptualising, when he is working his way through ideas and mental constructs which enable his to be creative and imaginative. As his imagination and creativity develop, he begins to experience the extensiveness of life. These experiences progress rapidly during this fifth 100-day period.

With this mental development, a child's emotional development is progressing concurrently. When he is unable to work his way through his emotional experiences during the daytime, then his subconscious will help him to process them during her night sleep. This will continue throughout life – we continue to experience dreams and nightmares, though not as often, as we grow into adulthood, when we manage to rationalise most of our emotions and anxieties at a higher level. Dreaming is the psyche's way of discharging the energies that are invested in our emotions and that have not been adequately discharged during our conscious awake time. Dreaming happens during our time of REM or light sleep when our body is unable to move and act out the dream. A nightmare is a frightening dream, but one that our consciousness is aware of. It can be remembered on waking.

A sleep terror is different to a nightmare and it occurs during a different part of the sleep cycle, during deep or non-REM sleep. Sleep terrors usually start to happen towards the end of a baby's first year, as a child's cognitive awareness and separation anxiety develops, and as the cyclic periods of deep sleep begin to lengthen and the periods of light sleep shortening proportionately. A sleep terror happens without awareness. It is not recollected on waking. If a child awakens from a sleep terror he may have only partial awareness. He may not even recognise you or his surroundings and may appear generally confused, have a rapid pulse and other signs of fear or anxiety, such as rapid breathing, gasping, moaning, crying and often screaming. He usually is able to settle back into quiet sleep straight away.

As a night terror occurs during a light stage of deep sleep, the body is not immobile and therefore the indications of a night terror may be that the child thrashes around or stands or calls out. As deep sleep naturally occurs during the first hours of sleeping, this is the time that sleep terrors happen more often. Nightmares, occurring during lighter REM sleep, generally happen towards the end of the early hours of the morning when there are longer periods of light sleep approaching the morning awakening. Night terrors become quite common in children from three to five years and then seem to decline.

Fears and anxieties, whether 'real' or not real, need to be validated. If a child is frightened, he is not being silly. He is being frightened and he does not need a reason for his fright. He needs reassurance, to be comforted and to be supported through his process. If he knows that he is surrounded by love and protection then he can gradually work through his feelings. This will stand him in good stead for the rest of his life. If his feelings are negated or dismissed, then he gains no sense of security and he will dread going to his bed. Bed needs to be a safe haven and a great place to be no matter what age we are.

If a child is going through a difficult nightmare period and is frightened to go to bed, then changing his bedroom set-up or the placing of his cot can help to reassure him. A nightlight or hallway light also helps, as does leaving his door open so that he can hear her family and have the reassurance of its presence. Identifying and alleviating his daytime anxieties and fears can also be a great support for him.

# FEEDING

A toddler doesn't need baby food anymore. He can have the food that his family is eating. However, he is a growing dynamo and he needs food to meet these needs. A toddler really hasn't got the time for anything except what he is doing *at the moment*. A toddler lives in the moment. He is being creative. Having to eat can be a nuisance. He therefore becomes a grazer, pecking here and there when he has hunger pangs.

A child can often exhibit hunger through irritable behaviour. He can drive his parents to distraction around food. Cooking him a soufflé is a waste of time. You'll only end up crying into it and then it is even more of a waste.

*A toddler's daily food requirements are: 1200 calories (quality calories):*
- *70% vegetables, fruits, grains, beans, pulses and seeds*
- *30% fish, meat, dairy products (or vegetarian/vegan equivalents) and added fats.*
- *Milk product – full cream milk, yoghurt, cheese, custard etc. – 500 ml.*
- *Red meat or fish or chicken or egg yolk or vegetarian equivalent in amounts that provide 10 mg iron/day*
  - *Vegetables – 5 servings*
  - *Fruit – 3 servings*

A parent's expectation is that their child will consume his food requirement. This doesn't always happen. If a child is a grazer or a snacker, then food snacks need to be nutritious. Supermarket toddler snacks are created to be addictive. Try to avoid them. Create your own.

One reason that a toddler may not have a hearty appetite during the day is that he is having vast quantities of milk, often at night. If a toddler has this pattern, then she can be weaned from it by reducing the quantities of milk by 10 ml per bottle per day and by watering down the milk 50 per cent. When the amount of milk is reduced to zero, then the habit can be broken, the bottles removed. If a child is having quantities of fruit juice, then his appetite will be greatly reduced. The only drink that a toddler requires is either milk or water. Juice and milk in a bottle encourages tooth decay. A toddler needs to be nursed in loving arms when he is drinking from a bottle.

Bottles (self-fed) in a toddler's bed are appetite distracters and lead to tooth decay also. It is a good idea to wean a toddler from drinking from a bottle by the time he is two years of age. At times of stressful situations for a toddler, such as the arrival of a new baby or a house move, removing his favourite comforts is not kind, so timing needs to be thought through. A feeding and weaning routine has been laid out in the previous third and fourth 100 days eating schedules.

## Creative Moments

A toddler from 14 to 18 months is totally self-absorbed. He knows that every person in the world and everything within his world is there for him – no sharing, no caring. He is the centre of the universe. And he is very busy. There is so much to be done, so many places to explore and lots of things to play with. The family kitchen, the local supermarket, all his toys and everybody else's toys as well, are there – just for him. The concept of ownership and sharing is not yet wired into this little person's brain. A little child of this age will spread himself through your life and he can weave magic while he is at it. It is a wonderful and yet sometimes frustrating time, not only for his family but also for him.

This period in a child's life is the awakening of creativity and communication. From jabbering at 14 months, he will go to attempting to sing when he is 18 months of age. He will also enjoy nursery rhymes and begin to join in with the recitation.

When an infant starts to walk, he takes uneven steps with feet wide apart attempting to maintain his balance by holding his arms slightly flexed above his head or at shoulder level. As he gains momentum, he looks as if he is in full flight until she plunges out of control into a heap. Sometimes it hurts, but this child has persistence and without a second thought he can get to his feet unaided and take off again. Stairs are a challenge and with sights set on conquering Everest, he is able to creep upstairs and carefully descend backwards.

Kneeling is a new trick, so being constrained in his pushchair or in the bath can be very challenging for him. When he gets close to 18 months of age, this child has progressed to walking well with his feet only slightly apart and he can stop and start with safety and control. He still tends to collide with obstacles along the way because his navigation is still immature. He is now able to push objects around while walking, though control of direction is still a little haphazard. However this child is getting there, wherever *there* is, and he is determined about it. Exploring his environment is still a priority for him.

His fine motor skills are also refining. He can place blocks on top of each other, building a tower of three blocks, and he can turn the pages of a book, several at a time.

He can take a spoon to his mouth without rotating his wrist and spilling the contents of the spoon. This is because there is greater maturity of the bones of the wrist, and this is dependent on the genetic inheritance of the child. The ossification of bones is dependent on, and a measure of, skeletal development and maturation. If there is slow development, it is probably because one or both of a child's parents were genetically slow developers. It is good to remember this and to reflect on how it was for his parents when they were at this stage of maturity. It enables us to understand and accept an individual child's milestones as he reaches them.

Sometimes milestones are advanced compared to the 'average', sometimes they are a little behind the average. We live in a world of comparisons, as if life is a race, and we then lose sight of individual achievements and the victory that lies within them.

The second year of a child's life is one of innate striving to achieve. To see an expression of pure joy on the face of a child who meets a milestone in his life is one of life's special moments.

This time is also the time of the birth of imagination. This ability comes with the development of conceptual skills, when a child is able to *have an idea* and to move through that idea in some sort of imaginative playacting. It is the beginning of learning life skills and of how to work a way through them in order to perfect them.

Little children, when asked about a particular situation, will relate it through the sequences of familiar events. Even before language skills have developed, we can observe toddlers between one and two years use imaginative play with toys to act out a sequence of familiar events. This imaginative stage of development is the start of moving towards being part of a bigger world that extends beyond the individual, which is the realisation that comes with the start of the next stage of a human shift in consciousness when a child is eight years of age.

Problem solving is part of developing conceptual and cognitive skills. Social skills develop with the development of language. Even though a child has been able to interact through means aside from spoken language up until this time, once words and sentences become part of his communication he is able to communicate conceptually, to ask questions, to process replies and to then develop social skills with individuals beyond his own family members. Language enables him to communicate with a wider world. It enables a child to learn the symbols of life and to use them for communication.

Memory is dependent on three facilities – recognition, recall and reconstruction of events or things in our life experiences. During this fifth 100-day period, as a child's brain continues its wiring and rewiring, he will begin to demonstrate his remembrance of past events. Recognition of people and things, through repeated stimulus, is quite joyful to watch. *Recognition* starts early in infancy whenever a previously experienced stimulus is repeated. It can be quite spontaneous and does not rely on long-term memory.

By the time this little child is four years old, his recognition memory is quite accurate because he has had a few years of repetitions of the same stimuli. During his second year, he encounters a lot of these stimuli because he is becoming a very sociable and inquisitive little person.

*Recall* is a little more sophisticated because it involves remembering a stimulus, such as a person, event or thing, that is not present. Even though recall is present towards the end of the child's first year, it becomes more evident in a child's second year through imaginative play. This is when a toddler will begin to act out some of your behaviours, the routines you carry out and your mannerisms. He begins to produce the mirror that shows you *you*. This can be a very revealing time for a parent, if not inspiring. As a child matures, he will recall events that occurred before he had even begun to have language.

*Reconstruction* is the process of remembering more complex events and stories and is beyond a toddler's ability. It is important to know this when we are guiding and teaching a toddler, because it enables us to check on our expectations of him.

Towards the end of this 100-day period, a child begins to show concern with any deviations from the way that things should be and the ways that people should act. He begins to notice 'damage' to clothes or objects and will point out a piece of dirt on a rug or in the bath. He begins to react with distress to aggressive behaviours that might endanger him or another's wellbeing. His language by the time he is two years of age will often express this as his vocabulary expands to include descriptive words, such as broken, hurt, dirty or 'uh-oh'. This little child is becoming a moral being.

From the age of about 17 months, a child notices deviations from what he regards as normal, whether it is a difference of a thing in the form of damage or deformation or a difference in behaviour in family members or peers. He is in tune with a rudimentary concept of cause and effect. He develops an ability to extract certain behaviours in those around him. He knows that if he does something noticeable, then Mummy or Daddy respond in a certain way. This is why, when a new sibling comes into his life, he will do anything to return his situation to the status quo – he learns that behaviour, whether 'good' or 'bad', attracts attention.

This need for attention is greater than her reasoning of how he gets it. If he does something, it doesn't matter how he does it so long as he gets attention. This way he can feel safe and secure and he can survive within his family group. It validates his existence and ensures his life survival.

Nothing achieves more than persistence. Nothing is created without persistence. Humans are creators, striving for new ways of doing things, new discoveries and new thoughts and concepts. This is how societies evolve.

When we see a child of this age at 'play', we are seeing a creative person with persistence and a growing vision, and this is what our world needs.

# PARENTING WITH COMMUNICATION AND CREATIVITY

To be a creative and communicative individual requires imagination and energy and patience. These qualities are also the requirements for the successful parenting of a child of 14 months to eight years of age. One of the best ways that we can do this is to reach in to our *own* inner little child and to recognise the frustrations that have arisen from our own stifled creativity. Knowing this can help us to understand the frustrated behaviour of a small child who is moving through what is described as 'two-year-old' behaviour. He does not have 'a tantrum', as his behaviour is often defined, he has a frustration. He just hasn't realised how to deal with his frustration without making a lot of noise.

How a frustration is dealt with all depends on an individual's level of maturity, an understanding of their own personal behaviour, the willingness and ability to modify their own behaviour and also their possession of life skills. Language skills are particularly important.

The throat energy centre is situated close to the surface of the body in a very vulnerable part of the neck. It is physically unprotected by bone or muscle structures, such as the skull, the ribcage, the strong musculature of the abdomen and the bony pelvis. It is the most vulnerable of all the energy centres of the body. And yet it is through this centre that we can be most in touch with our inner child, the energetic part of us that determines our adult behaviour.

The centre of anything controls the outer parts. The core energy of any matter is the strongest energy. The apple seed determines the fruit, its form, its strength, its nutritional value and its expression – its flavour. If the apple seed is not nurtured in its early growth, then the fruit will be stunted in one or all of its qualities.

The apple seed is contained in the core of the fruit. Our *own* inner child is like the apple seed and it needs to be nurtured. Our world is determined and consumed by outward appearances, and we now tend to deny the inner person of us. The inner person is the child that we were and who we are now. The inner person is our essence and it is our source. Our inner person is in fact our inner child who is nourished by our environment, how we recognise and acknowledge it, how we nurture it and how we heal it. It is time to look into the mirror, because our inner child is the core of understanding the part of us who feels, thinks and responds in the same way that we did in our childhood.

When we feel an emotion such as rage, sadness, hurt or fear, or we have a feeling of being denied or lost or betrayed or empty when we are adults, we are usually feeling an emotion that has hurt us as a child. These feelings are stimulated by something that happened way back in our history. It is good to recognise this, so that in adulthood we can work with our emotions without dumping them on others through inappropriate expression.

Because this energy centre is so exposed to outside forces, it gives and receives energy without filtering or protection, and this is particularly so when we are children. There was an old Victorian proverb which said that 'children should be seen and not heard'. How did you feel about not being heard when you were a little child? How do you feel about not being heard in adulthood?

The feeling of not being heard as a child determines how we react when we feel, as an adult, that we are not being heard. And we can *over*react or we can *under*-react, depending on how we learnt to deal with the situation of not being heard as a child. The important thing is that we recognise the feeling and, if we are able, recognise where it came from, the way that we dealt with and thought about it as a child, and how we as an adult deal with, think about and express the feeling now.

Everything, every event in the life of a child is big. The family home, the school playground, even the school bully, was big. A very humbling experience is to revisit these experiences as adults. Can you revisit your childhood home, the street where it is, your old infants school, and get a feeling of you as a little child? This can kindle your memories and awaken your imagination. And you will see through your adult eyes that, really and relatively, your beginnings were smaller than what you have remembered them as.

It also provides a metaphor for an event we remember from our childhood. When we were children, the happenings in our life were big, but if we question our family about them they might not even remember them.

In adulthood a childhood event is still big in our memory because the impact that it had on us was *big*. The emotion that we had around the event was big, and it still is, because it is so deeply imbedded within our memory which is sometimes subconscious. This is the event's importance – it has been laid down in memory, which exists in every cell of the body although it is the mind that processes it and articulates it. For this reason, it is good to seek counsel so that the energy around the memory can be released.

The act of putting the memory into language is a way of diffusing it, of working through it so that the energy that the memory contains can be turned into positive and healing energy. Language is a healing gift. If it is the spoken word, the energy around the words is released on the breath. If we commit the memory to paper by writing it out, we are able to see the word and process its truth. This is why journal writing or 'morning pages' are such releasing activities.

All adults in our childhood were big, towering over us, exerting their power and diminishing ours and sometimes even laughing at our creativity and what we saw as our achievements. It can be crushing for a little child, but most of the time adults do not realise what they are doing because they are merely unconsciously repeating their own childhood experiences. This is why, as adults, we need to develop a consciousness of our own actions. And we need to be not so *big* to a child.

The sweetest way to engage with a child is to get down to her level. Actually kneel or squat down on our haunches, so that our eyes are meeting a child's eyes at her height – it is amazing to realise how *our* communication changes and softens and it is so much easier to meet your child. Not only the little child with whom you are communicating with, but also with your own inner little child. This is the safest way to be – as a child – with equality and without threat.

Congruence is the fact or condition of agreeing. When we think of congruence in terms of behaviour it means that our words and our actions agree.

To have congruence in what we say and what we do, we need to have and to maintain our own *personal integrity* in all dealings with others. Personal integrity is the act of following through with our commitments. If we say that we will do something, or we make a promise to do so, then we need to uphold or keep this commitment. This is especially true in our dealings with children. To break our promise or commitment to our child is devastating for the child, and is long remembered.

We are social beings with social needs or values. The development of morality is based on the promotion of thought and behaviour – acts of 'social cognition'. *Social intelligence* or social skills is a function of moral development. The growth process of socialisation involves both moral development and cognitive development, both of which are evident in a child of 18 months. Little children learn through example. If they see the adults in their life demonstrate empathy, conscience, self-control, respect, kindness, tolerance and fairness in their actions, then they can absorb and emulate this behaviour. Little children love to conform to the norm of their families and then, as they grow into middle childhood at the age of seven or eight years, to their peer group. Their early learning of moral behaviour begins in their home environment. Careful guidance and explanation is essential for this learning.

Parenting with integrity demands the highest honesty. Actions are the communicators. Little children watch very carefully and what they see within their home becomes their standard and what they take out into society. Teaching a child the golden rule that has guided many civilisations behoves us to live our life by it as well.

The golden rule is: *Treat others as you yourself want to be treated.*

We are all innately creative beings but for some there is a personal belief that they are not creative people. We have come to believe that creativity is associated only with artistic or musical or dextrous ability and unless we produce a piece of 'brilliant' artwork or music or literature or craft, then we are not creative people. But we need to listen to our language and when and how we use the word 'create'. We speak of creating peace or creating havoc, creating a safe environment, creating a home and creating a new idea. It's all about making 'something' happen. That 'something' can contribute to the welfare of the planet and of humankind. It can also be an incredibly destructive force.

The creativity of this energy centre is the *expression* of the creativity of the second energy centre. Svadisthana is the source of our creative ability and its desire. The third energy (solar plexus) centre provides the drive for this ability.

The heart centre, Anahata, provides the love that makes the creation beautiful, but it is this fifth energy centre, Vishudda, that brings the creation to full expression.

Little children never doubt their creative ability. They paint their pictures, they sing their songs, they make mud cakes and sand castles and they dance and they love – all with great self-assurance and without question. Little children believe in themselves and their creativity. When do we lose the belief that we had in ourselves and in our creative ability? At what stage is it snuffed out of us? And why? Where does it go?

In the myth of Hercules and the Cretan bull, Minos broke his promise to Poseidon that he would sacrifice the bull to the gods. Instead he kept the creature for himself. He denied the bull's creative purpose through sacrifice.

Life is not life if it is without symbolic death or sacrifice. Often through our lifespan we need to sacrifice or give up a part of us in order to move onto a new stage of growth. Each beat of our heart does this – about 70 times in each minute the heart fills with blood and releases it with the pulse of life and death. In so doing, it maintains life. In order for the hand to take up and hold something, it first needs to surrender and release what it is holding on to. In order to develop a new behaviour, we need to let go of the old one.

When we begin to compare ourselves with our peers, we tend to focus on the material things of life, the things that we can gain in order to fill the void left by our lost creative talent. Also through comparing ourself to our peers, we can feel humbled to the point of incapacity – we just don't feel good enough by comparison and we lose sight of our will and our special abilities and talents. We, like the Cretan bull, go out and wreak havoc because we lose sight of the beauty of our self. Minos denied the bull the right to fulfil its creative purpose.

We lose our beautiful creativity when we lose a belief in our own self. To regain our sense of self, we need to recreate our creativity. Attend drawing classes, sing or learn a musical instrument. Take a photo, create and maintain a garden, create a beautiful meal. What is it, deep inside of you, that you would like to create?

The throat energy centre contains, maintains and delivers our voice. If we withhold our words, we become meek and shy. The chin lowers over our throat in a withholding timid stance and our self-esteem withers. To be proud and to stand tall, we need to reclaim our confidence, to choose our words carefully so that they give rather than take away.

It is amazing how our body reflects our mind and the mind reflects our body through what is known as 'body language'. If we develop an upright posture, lengthen our neck to hold our head high, straighten our shoulders and stand with our feet firmly planted apart and parallel on the ground, then we can gain confidence in how we are in the world and know that our voice is valid and worthy of being heard. Maintaining eye contact with whomever we are conversing means keeping our head up and speaking our truth. This is honest communication. We expect the truth from others and they are deserving of ours. Eye contact while we are communicating is in itself a communication.

There are times, sometimes many times in a day, that our negative feelings rise up from the lower energy centres – fear, sadness, anger, spite can cause havoc if not checked by this throat centre. If you feel your Cretan bull getting ready to unleash itself, excuse yourself, find a pillow or cushion or towel and scream, growl or bellow into it. Releasing the energy from these feelings into a 'noise' cushion feels so good that the words soften and the truth emerges in correct form. Teach your child how to do this too. It is the beginning of learning a life skill. And it is also about taking responsibility for our actions and words, owning our feelings and dealing with them in an appropriate way.

To be an effective communicator requires our congruence and our integrity. It requires speaking our heart and our mind. It is also about learning how to feel with the mind and to think with the heart. It is, in its own way, a creative skill. Very little children know no other way – they are born to think with their heart. If we speak about our personal role in an event, and how we feel, and how we see and hear the event, then we are speaking our truth.

To speak our truth, we need to be able to say the word 'no' when that is what we really want to say. So often, when we are asked to do or give of something, we say 'yes' when what we really want to say is 'no'. Doing this fractures our personal integrity, we feel resentful and it is not honest communication. Learning to say 'no' when that is what we really want to say does take practice, but the honesty of it earns respect from others and strengthens our self-esteem. If at first this is confronting, then saying *I need to think about it* does give us time to think about why, in the circumstance, it is so difficult to say 'no'. This is self-awareness and it lifts our personal self-esteem.

It is speaking our truth.

*If you bring forth what is within you, what you bring forth will save you. If you do not bring forth what is within you, what you do not bring forth will destroy you.*

GOSPEL OF ST THOMAS: LOGION 45

# SECTION III
## Self-responsibility

# THE CHILD OF
# EIGHT YEARS

# AJNA
## *The Third Eye Chakra*

# INTRODUCTION

The first seven years of a child's life are known as 'the formative years' and they provide the foundation for the growth and maturity that comes with the consciousness awakened through higher learning and the search for spiritual meaning in our life.

The awakening of the first three energy centres ground us in survival skills, creativity and strength of the will. The heart and throat centres allow us to feel and express our emotions and start to truly interact with the world around us. As a child achieves these developmental milestones, she is moving into the realms of the more esoteric or spiritual centres – Ajna, the third eye chakra and Sahasrara, the crown chakra.

The sixth and seventh energy centres take us into the realms of the mind where we are able to synthesise our life experiences and to recognise and accept our divine nature. Life becomes an inner journey. Saint Ignatius of Loyola, founder of the Jesuits, said: *Give me a child until the age of seven and I will show you the man.* The formative years do to some degree determine our outlook on life.

The sixth energy centre, commonly known as the third eye, begins to flower in a child of about eight years of age and marks the time of transition from the period of life when basic conceptual and cognitive skills are developed to a life of higher learning and the search for the *meaning* of life.

It marks the beginning of conscious awareness.

A symbolic lotus of two petals, Ajna gives us intuition, which is rich, active and receptive during the first two months after birth when the brain has not yet developed its receptive communicative abilities. The intuitive centre of Ajna becomes less dominant as we listen less to our centre of inner knowing and focus on the mental skills that come as the brain matures and grows in its willing acceptance of cognition, conceptualising skills and a gaining of language as our main means of external communication. It is during this time that we can become right- or left-brain dominant.

In our western culture we tend to deny our right-brain intuitive and creative development in favour of our left-brain rational and analytical development.

Within each of the two petals of the lotus there are 48 radiating spokes and together they amount to 96 segments or 'petals', which represent the 96 months of the life of a child in her eighth year. This age marks the beginning development of a child's ability to have insight, complex thought and to develop and possess self-awareness.

The first of the higher centres, this energy centre stirs in the eighth year of life and continues its flowering through adolescence and adulthood, just as the centres that have prepared for its growth will continue their development.

This centre flowers in the getting of wisdom and it is in the getting of wisdom that we find our true purpose in life. It enables a consciousness that reaches beyond each one of us as individuals and also where we develop unity with our own inner 'being'.

We have a great capacity to tap into our intuitive abilities and to synthesise our life experiences. We can view our experiences as learning opportunities and turn them into positive visualisations for now and for the future. When we can do this, we not only heal ourselves but we facilitate the healing of others and also the healing of our world.

# The Sixth Energy Centre

AJNA

'Choice'

## *The Lotus of Two Petals*

A Child of Eight Years

Consciousness

COLOUR: Indigo, the deep blue of the early night sky. The colour of introspection, its influence takes us away from the world of the mundane towards more
spiritual dimensions.

MUSIC: European classical music, including art, concert and orchestral music, which enable higher brain function. All the sonatas created by Mozart are particularly associated with this energy centre. European classical music developed within a philosophy of the era of the Enlightenment, which placed an emphasis on the natural rights of people and on the ability of humans to shape their own environment. Simplicity, balance and an interest in real emotions were critical for its composers.

SENSE: Sixth sense, which is extrasensory perception or inner knowing.

PHYSICAL SYSTEM: The eyes, base of skull and hypothalamus.

ENDOCRINE GLAND: Pituitary gland.

ANIMAL TOTEM: There is no animal totem for this centre as it is not concerned with earthly or tangible aspects of life.

# AJNA – CONSCIOUSNESS
## 'TO PERCEIVE AND TO COMMAND'

Ajna is situated deep within the brain, just above the base of the skull. Externally it is at a point above the eyes and between the eyebrows. It is referred to as the third eye – it gives us insight and the ability to visualise, it is the mind's eye.

Ajna marks the age of intellectual learning and it is truly open and receptive in our middle age, when its enhanced energy spurs us to ask of our self *What is the purpose of my life?* We reach a time of questioning our existence, of searching for the meaning of our life and of formulating the answers into a life path. Many individuals find their own inner knowing only after an adulthood period of not seeing it.

The symbolic representation of Ajna is a lotus of two petals and within each petal there are 48 spokes or rays. In my view, each of the two petals is the representation of each of the two hemispheres of the brain, with the seedpod within representing the pituitary gland, the corpus callosum, the optic chiasma (crossing) and the hypothalamus. Each petal reflects the qualities of each hemisphere of the brain – the male, rational and analytic left-brain, and the female, creative and artistic right brain. This energy centre brings the two together so that there is no longer a duality of thought but a melding into the whole. It enables holistic thought.

Ajna is the centre of intuitive thought, imagination and clairvoyance.

The sacramental association of this centre is ordination, the ceremony that invokes the powers needed to become one who works to bring peace through union of the physical (mundane) and spiritual aspects of humans.

The elemental association of this centre is light – without light we would not have sight. When light reaches the retina of the eye the receptors of the retina relay the signals of light via the optic nerve to the visual area of the brain, which then converts the impulses into images of what we 'see'.

Ajna is the centre of the fourth dimension – the dimension of time. Albert Einstein in 1921 introduced time as the fourth dimension in his theory of relativity, which states that space cannot be separated from time, and that time is affected by the presence of matter flowing at different rates through different parts of the universe. The fourth dimension is an expression occasionally used to describe something beyond the limits of normal experience. The source of time is the mind. Time is a concept which humans use as a measure of where we have been in the past and where we will be in the future. The present or the now is not part of time. We are *within* the now and it cannot be measured. Little children have no concept of time – they exist in the *now*, and it is interesting to note that the analogue clock is not taught in school until a child is eight years of age. Time is an abstract concept and a small child does not have the capacity to grasp abstracts until this centre begins to flower at about eight years of age.

In the practice of meditation there is a transcendence of the three-dimensional world of clocks, and the mind enters into a fourth dimension where time and space are irrelevant to anything else. It has been observed that those who regularly meditate can achieve youthfulness through the slowing down of their body processes.

Eastern mysticism has developed a strong inner knowing of the reality of space-time, believing that both space and time are inseparably linked – that they exist within each other. In the same way it is believed that the body, the mind, the spirit and the emotions are interpenetrating and cannot exist without each other.

Our thoughts create our reality, how we are in the world and the choices we make within it. A decision or choice is made when we 'make up our mind'.

Physically, Ajna is situated at the base of the brain and involves the eyes, the hypothalamus and the occipital and temporal lobes of the cerebral hemispheres, all parts of us that enable sight.

The main bones which make up the base of the skull, the part that cradles the base of the brain, are the sphenoid bone, the ethmoid bone, the temporal bones and the occipital bone which support the occipital lobes of the brain.

It is the sphenoid bone that holds a special place in the base of the skull. It is called the keystone of the cranial floor because it articulates with all the other cranial bones, holding them together. Shaped like an outstretched butterfly, the sphenoid bone stretches between both temples.

A temple is a place of worship, an edifice erected to a deity or any place said to be occupied by the Divine Presence. The sphenoid bone is worthy of this metaphor for within it is a small protected opening, where resides one of the most powerful glands in our bodies, the pituitary gland.

The hypothalamus is located just below the thalamus and above the pituitary gland. This very small area of the brain is the main regulator of homeostasis, which is the state in which the body's internal environment remains in balance. It has an amazing number of functions, the main ones being: control of the autonomic nervous system and the pituitary gland; the regulation of eating and drinking; body temperature and diurnal (day) rhythms, and states of consciousness – sleep and wakefulness. Together with the limbic system, the hypothalamus regulates our emotional and behavioural patterns, such as feelings of rage, aggression, pain and pleasure, and the behavioural patterns of sexual arousal.

The hypothalamus is believed to be the master of the pituitary gland and is associated with the pursuit of pleasure and our learnt and instinctive moral and ethical behaviour. The hypothalamus is a crucial endocrine gland, producing at least nine different hormones and it is also the major integrating link between the nervous system and the endocrine system.

The hypothalamus receives input from several other regions of the brain. It also receives sensory signals from internal organs and the visual system. Therefore any painful, stressful or emotional experience can cause changes in its activity as it controls the autonomic nervous system and regulates body temperature, thirst, hunger, sexual behaviour and defensive reactions such as fear and rage. It can be regarded as the *growth* regulator of the body.

It can also be considered as the seat of our conscience.

Ajna is the centre of command, which is not the command of others but rather the command of our self, our personal growth and our knowledge in life.

The associated endocrine gland is the pituitary gland, which is regarded as the master gland, commanding all other glands of the body's endocrine system. However it has this command only with the higher command of the hypothalamus, the part of the brain situated about 5 to 8 centimetres behind the midpoint between the eyes.

Emotionally, *Ajna* regulates our emotional responses. This centre is the one where we choose our responses to life situations. If we allow ourselves to experience an emotion, we can express it through the other energy centres via verbal expression, touch or action. If we suppress an emotional feeling, it is then stored in the subconscious where in its original form it becomes blocked or deadened and from where it can be expressed through inappropriate behaviour that we are often unaware of.

Ajna is our emotional point of choice.

Mentally, this energy centre is where our life attitudes are formulated. It is also the area of reason, analysis and evaluation with which we perceive and 'work out' our world. It is our mind centre, where we develop our understanding of self and of others. This is the centre of personal choices and personal growth. We can choose to modify and develop our own behaviour. When this centre is balanced and at ease, then we can be at peace with ourselves and with others. If it is not in balance, then there is mental turmoil, our thoughts cannot be still, and sleep and peace of mind are not available to us.

Precognition is the understanding or receiving of information by extra-sensory means. This centre is where we develop our inner knowing – our *intuition*. Often this knowing can be revealed through the practice of meditation.

Ajna is our centre of meditation.

Spiritually, Ajna is our centre of self-command and wisdom, which comes with the maturity of age. It is in this centre that we develop our personal code of ethics, form our belief systems, question the 'rights' and 'wrongs' of the world we live in and develop our perception of a fourth dimension of all things. It is the seeing beyond the physical, emotional and mental aspects of all things because it is from this centre that we are able to view all things from a holistic perspective.

The element of this centre is light. It is the light of the world, the sight of our eyes, the light that shines on our understanding, when we *see the light* and we are able to 'spread the light' which is the illumination of our own wisdom. When we withhold our soul essence we do not share our self on a deep level with others, and we are denying our self and others the right and pleasure of sharing our wisdom. To 'hide our light under a bushel' is to conceal our talents, and to be self-effacing and modest about our abilities. Opening the door to the light within can only be done from within. Light is a metaphor for the spirit and the divinity, symbolising inner enlightenment. It is also our intelligence.

Light is the most basic symbol of conscious life.

*Once you make a decision, the universe conspires to make it happen.*

RALPH WALDO EMERSON.

# THE BEHAVIOUR OF A PERCEPTIVE CHILD

In the first two years, during the *sensorimotor* stage of development, a child learns through her senses – smell, taste, vision, touch and hearing. Physical development, particularly of the brain, enables her motor or movement development. Through her senses and ability to move and manipulate her immediate environment, she absorbs information about her world and the people in it. She does not have a lot of *self*-awareness.

During early childhood, from two to seven years of age, a child moves through the *preoperational* stage of development when she is able to represent her experiences through thought and language. Language begins to develop in the second year but there is a phenomenal growth in its facility from the age of two. Mental representation, where an infant can sustain an internal image of an absent object or a past event, becomes more sophisticated as language skills mature during the end of the second year and into the third year. A child, through receiving a basic explanation, can mentally visualise an object or event.

Language is the most flexible way of mental representation. When we think in words, we can begin to understand our world through internal processes or our creative imagination, rather than through our basic senses and actions.

Make-believe play develops from the early stages of imitation to a fantasy stage of play, when life gets played out with dolls and toy trucks and dress-up clothes as well as objects that can represent other objects. The child learns to think and act out her world through symbols. A gumnut may represent a cup, a broken branch may represent a sword or a broom or even a horse to ride. The substitute object is the symbol and it allows for the development of the concept of representation.

The child also begins to play through reverse roles – imitating her parents, or the doctor or nurse or fireman, and using substitute people, teddy bears, dolls, other children to complete the scene. She might say to an adult, 'I'll be the mummy and you are all my children.' Little children begin to learn parenting through this type of play. They believe their fantasy, declaring that when they grow up they are going to be a fireman or a nurse or a spaceman. She may also create an imaginary friend.

The child's pencil and drawing skills are developing. She learns the symbols of language, the letters that make words and numbers and also how to put them together to create meaning. As cognitive and fine motor skills become more refined, a child brings more realism into her drawings, and when she develops the ability to draw lines to create boundaries for the objects that she has drawn then this drawing becomes more complex, though not necessarily realistic. Imagination still fuels creation and the idea of copying or recreating their own work or the work of another is not considered.

Young children pass through several phases of understanding, including logical reasoning, until the eighth year when they become more adaptable to their formal education. They begin to understand the views of others in simple familiar situations and in everyday communication. They can distinguish animate beings from inanimate objects and begin to see that magic does not change everyday experiences. They begin to categorise objects through their common function and the kind of object that it is, and they can classify familiar objects into groups.

From four to seven years, children begin to use plausible explanations for the cause and effect of different situations, rather than relying on magical thinking. They are capable of *reverse thinking* by working their way back through an event, and are able to explain, through the natural idea of cause and effect, the reasons for familiar situations such as when they are asked to give their account of any situation that they have been involved in. They also show an improved ability to distinguish appearance from reality: that what they think has happened may not be the real situation.

Middle childhood spans the years from eight to 12. These are the years of new consciousness when the sixth energy centre begins to blossom. During these years, children begin to think in a more organised, logical fashion about concrete, tangible information. They show improved understanding of spatial concepts – the meaning of time and an improved idea of distances. They do not continue to ask 'are we there yet' when travelling. This marks a great leap in their ability to tolerate longer journeys from home. They begin to develop a clearer concept of time and to interpret it within other concepts, such as distance, birthdays and celebrations. They are also able to receive and interpret clear directions and explanations and also to give them to others.

# MENTAL DEVELOPMENT

The brain and nervous system has two major growth spurts. These involve the development of new brain cell connections, which contribute to increases in the thickness of the cerebral cortex or grey matter. The first growth spurt, which occurs between six and eight years of age, occurs in the motor and sensory areas of the brain. This growth is reflected in the refinement of fine motor skills and eye-hand co-ordination. The second growth spurt happens after the age of eight, mainly in the frontal lobes of the cerebral cortex. These areas govern logic and planning, which are the two cognitive functions that mature rapidly during this period.

*Selective attention* is the ability to focus thinking on the *important* elements of a problem or situation and relegate low priority to the less important details. As nerve connections between the reticular formation and the frontal lobes of the brain become more fully insulated, children begin to function more like adults when they need to focus on the necessary elements of a situation. There is an increased rate of insulation of nerve connections between the neurons of the areas of the brain where sensory and motor and intellectual functions are located. This contributes to greater skill and speed in the processing of information.

*Spatial cognition* is the ability to identify and act on relationships between objects in space. It enables the ability to read maps, to imagine how people and objects can be moved around within a space and to visualise the result. Understanding the concept of *right* and *left* develops at the same time. Visual experience plays an important part in this aspect of brain development. At this age, boys and girls demonstrate differences in their abilities. Boys score much higher in this area than girls and this could be the result of boys having a greater interest in constructing activities such as building with blocks during play in their early and middle childhood.

*Spatial perception* is related to mathematical achievement and learning. So is the learning and appreciation of classical music. This is why it has been traditional for children to learn a musical instrument and to develop the ability to read notated music. The use of video games also contributes to this skill, but the overuse of these games can lead to debilitating social and emotional loss. It is all a question of balance – a healthy, balanced mix of activities.

At school a child's readiness to learn depends on her experience in life. Parental encouragement of their child's learning is essential. Rewarding children with enthusiasm, warmth and praise for putting in their very best effort ensures their steady educational progress and prepares them to use their intelligence and knowledge productively.

# Learning

*Literacy*, the ability to read and write, is the focus of education in the middle childhood years. This process, which started in early childhood education, continues until a child goes to secondary school. Children also learn the language of mathematics and more fully develop the ability to 'think' – to translate formal learning into practical life.

There is more than one pathway to learning. There are children who have a very strong innate visual pathway of learning and functioning. There are others whose learning and functioning pathway is aurally stronger – they have very keen hearing and listening skills. Then there are those who learn kinaesthetically, through 'doing', intuiting and experiencing the way that they learn and function in life.

We all have a dominant pathway but it does not mean that we cannot learn through other ways. It is important to understand that there are different pathways of learning and functioning in life and to understand and accommodate the child in her dominant facility. Our understanding can then lead to recognition and strengthening of the pathways that are not dominant and enhancing the innate dominant pathway.

Formal schooling has not always helped in this, but if parents can understand then they are better able to help their child build the skills that she will need in his life. Natural talent or intelligence can be recognised and reinforced.

In 1983 the psychologist Howard Gardner, who questioned the idea that intelligence is a single entity, proposed a theory of multiple intelligences.

*Linguistic intelligence* is the ability to use language, both spoken and written, effectively. It is also the ability to learn languages. Writers, poets, lawyers and speakers possess high linguistic intelligence.

*Logical-mathematical intelligence* consists of the ability to analyse problems logically, to carry out mathematical operations and to investigate issues scientifically. This entails an ability to detect patterns, to reason deductively and to think logically. This intelligence is most often associated with scientific and mathematical thinking.

*Musical intelligence* involves skill in the performance, composition and appreciation of musical patterns.

*Bodily-kinaesthetic intelligence* entails the potential of using one's whole body or parts of the body to solve problems. It is the ability to use mental abilities to co-ordinate bodily movements. Gardner recognises mental and physical activity as related. Outstanding athletes have this intelligence as do those who have physical co-ordination and dexterity, using fine and gross motor skills and expressing themselves or learning through physical activities. Actors, dancers and those who use various kinds of manipulative skills to solve problems or to learn have this intelligence.

*Spatial intelligence* involves the potential to recognise and use the patterns of wide space and more confined areas. Architects and landscape gardeners and graphic artists would be regarded as having strong spatial intelligence.

*Interpersonal intelligence* is concerned with the capacity to understand the intentions, motivations and desires of other people. Nurses, teachers, sociologists and perhaps all of those who are engaged in the caring professions have strength in this area.

*Intrapersonal intelligence* entails the capacity to understand oneself, to appreciate one's feeling, fears and motivations. People who have a strong capacity to regulate their own lives and to recognise and positively accept their own strengths with determination have intrapersonal intelligence.

In 1996, Gardner added another intelligence to the list – *naturalist intelligence*, which is the intelligence that has to do with observing, understanding and organising patterns in the natural environment. Biologists, zoologists and environmentalists are strong in this intelligence. Rachel Carson and Charles Darwin are good examples.

These eight intelligences do not work in isolation – there is cohesion with them all. However, we all have strong intelligence in certain areas and weaknesses in others. Orthodox education methods have had narrow pathways and those who cannot attain excellence in those particular skills have been deemed to not be 'intelligent'. Howard Gardner's work has revealed a new way of assessment and understanding for educators and also for individuals who do not 'fit' into standard boxes of degrees of intelligence. Other intelligences are now being recognised.

We are all intelligent beings – this is part of being human – but 'intelligence' has had such a narrow definition many children and adults have never had the opportunity to express their unique abilities. It is important to understand that Gardner's theory of multiple intelligences allows for multiple ways of *teaching*. It also allows for an acceptance that children (and adults) think and learn in many different ways and that people are not 'dumb' just because they don't think and learn in the way that society demands that they should do so.

To live life well, all intelligences are needed. Formal education places great emphasis on linguistic intelligence and logical-mathematical intelligence. However, once a child's individual intelligence strength is recognised, family and societal input is needed to make up for the shortfall of the child's academic schooling. Without positive family and societal recognition, input and acceptance, a child soon learns that she is 'not good enough', 'dumb' or that she doesn't measure up, with a resulting lifetime of low self-esteem. Sometimes a child may be 'slow' to realise a concept, but once she does understand it, she is often better able to apply it in the real world than the child who has worked it all out very quickly.

Understanding and knowledge is worth much more if it is *practically* applied rather than only stored in memory for the purpose of tests and examinations.

# PHYSICAL DEVELOPMENT

Physical development from six to 12 years is steady and slow. During middle childhood, children grow 5 to 8 centimetres and gain on average 2.5 kilograms each year. Their large muscle coordination is becoming more refined and is reflected in their abilities with sports and bike riding, not only in their strength but also in their control. Hand, foot and eye co-ordination is reflected in greater ball sport skills. Fine motor skills are also more refined and are reflected in greatly improved pencil skills in drawing and writing and abilities with computer games.

Sex differences in bone and skeletal maturation can lead boys and girls to pursue different activities. During the middle years, many children enter puberty. Knowledge of the life cycle and human reproductive biology is essential for them to embrace many of the changes that are happening within them and their friends. Developing a sense of responsibility for personal health, including dental health, has its foundations in middle childhood years.

Girls mature faster than boys. They reach, on average, 50 per cent of their adult height at about four and a half years of age compared with five and a half years in boys; they enter puberty earlier and they stop growing at an earlier age than boys. The difference in the onset of puberty accounts for boys having nearly two years extra pre-adolescent body growth than girls who enter puberty earlier than boys. Consequently, boys in the pre-adolescent years change proportions to become longer legged, relative to total height, than girls, accounting for their greater height in adulthood. It all depends on this growth during the last middle childhood years.

Puberty means sexual maturity and originally the term was applied to the appearance of pubic hair. 'Puberty' now refers to the period when the sex organs begin to enlarge during the later middle childhood years.

Physical growth throughout life is not only influenced by heredity and social environment but also the healthy functioning of the endocrine system, particularly the pituitary gland under the direction of the hypothalamus. The pituitary gland and the hypothalamus regulate virtually all aspects of physical growth, development, metabolism and homeostasis. Growth hormone is abundant in the human pituitary gland with levels 1000 times higher than any other pituitary hormone. Even though growth hormone levels in the blood are constantly low, at irregular intervals eight or nine times every 24 hours (more during night sleep) the levels rise sharply for ten to 20 minutes. Growth hormone secretion is increased by exercise and anxiety. It is also responsible for the growth of muscles. While there is an increased release of growth hormone during puberty, physical growth is also dependent on other hormones such as thyroid hormone and the sex hormones. When we are born we come with a full complement of nerve and muscle cells. As the body develops, nerve and muscle cells mature, and in the case of muscle cells, increase in size, thereby accounting for greater muscle mass, particularly in boys.

Major brain growth spurts occur during the middle childhood years and again in adolescence at about 15 years of age. A growth spurt in early adulthood occurs during the ages of 18 to 20 years. These growth spurts involve development of new brain cell connections as well as increases in the thickness of the cerebral cortex or grey matter.

A child of six to eight years has improvements in fine motor skills (dexterity) and greater eye-hand coordination. During the second growth spurt, from ten to 12 years of age, there is increased development of the *frontal lobes* of the cerebral cortex. The frontal lobes develop thought processes such as insight, memory and decision making, as well as guide our responses to emotional messages and help us to organise information.

At about nine years of age there is further development of the occipital lobes, which increase the child's capacities in logic and planning and greater abilities in visual-spatial perception, especially in tasks such as map reading. Myelination (insulation) of nerve connections also continues throughout middle childhood, contributing to greater concentration and focusing abilities. This ability leads to the particular type of concentration called *selective attention*, which enables a child to discern the important factors of a situation, thereby more easily reaching solutions in problem solving.

Adolescence is the transition period between puberty and adulthood – it is the final stage of childhood and is often used to describe the psychological and behavioural changes of this time. Some children do not begin their adolescent development until other children are completing it. There is a strong hereditary link to the onset of puberty and adolescence. Knowing the family history of maturation can help parents to make decisions about their child's schooling progress, when to allow their child to progress to higher levels and when to check that progress.

There is a link between early and late physical maturing, mental ability and emotional development, and this can have a profound impact on how a child copes with her peer group and the pressures that the group applies, particularly in the realm of self-esteem, the development of leadership skills and also in sporting performance.

Emotional attitudes are closely related to the physiological events that happen in a child's life and ultimately influence adulthood behaviours. Boys particularly are affected by their own physical abilities – physical prowess brings prestige and success. Girls also are affected by late development but in a different way – body image and sexual abilities are related to how they view their obvious physical development, their breasts, and ultimately to their fears of not being attractive and capable. However, early maturing girls can feel very self-conscious and embarrassed about their developing breasts and their increased fat gains, with an accompanying confusion around their early sex drives.

Studies have shown that late maturing boys show more attention-getting behaviour with their peers, and are less popular with lower social status than the early maturer.

The increase of skeletal muscle size is greater in boys than girls and at the end of middle childhood it rapidly escalates, due to the increase in male sex hormone. Boys also develop larger hearts, larger lungs, a greater capacity for carrying oxygen in the blood and a greater ability to neutralise the chemical products of muscular exercise. Boys in puberty become more adapted to tasks that require physical strength – a necessary requirement for the male of the species for hunting, fighting and lifting heavy objects. Consequently, pubescent boys develop greater changes in athletic ability than do girls.

## EMOTIONAL DEVELOPMENT

Up to the age of about seven or eight years a child will view and describe another person in terms of physical characteristics. For example, if a young child is asked to describe a friend, she will give a description of the colour of his eyes, hair, skin; whether he is tall, thin and where he lives. After the child enters middle childhood, she will begin to view and to describe other people in terms of abstract observation and her own personal assessment of them. 'He smells OK, he runs fast, he's really good (cool) at some particular activity and he loves music or dogs and lives in a big family with lots of brothers and sisters, and also he is kind.'

Behavioural qualities are described in comparative terms, and peak at about eight years then decline. Psychological constructs, or the way that the child sees 'the inner being' of her peer, will continue to become more sophisticated throughout middle childhood. There is a growing emphasis throughout middle childhood on the internal rather than the external characteristics on how a child views others.

Social relationships shift and change during middle childhood. As the child grows towards adolescence, while still being very attached to parents, she is moving towards independence, with disciplinary interactions with parents beginning to decline. She begins to make autonomous decisions around her social life and actions and negotiates her household tasks in terms of allowances.

Relationships with siblings are not as important to this child as are her relationships with parents and friends.

There are different kinds of sibling relationships. There is the *caregiver* relationship, where an older sibling will serve as a kind of quasi-parent to a younger sibling. There is the *buddy* relationship, where two siblings try to emulate each other and take pleasure in the company of each other. There is the *critical* relationship, where there is conflict when one sibling will try to dominate another with teasing and quarrelling. The *rival* relationship is similar to the critical relationship but it lacks any form of friendliness or support. A *casual* relationship is one in which the siblings have relatively little to do with one another.

## The development of empathy

Empathy is the 'in-feeling' that one has when touched by another's emotions. It is the ability to understand the feelings of another person and respond with complementary emotions. Empathy requires awareness of the feelings of another person and the ability to respond to those feelings with similar feelings. It also requires an ability to perceive *different* emotions in another person. Empathy has its beginnings in infancy when a baby will express the unexpressed emotions of its mother. If a mother holds back tears, then her baby will usually express them through crying and unsettled behaviour. The baby does not process this through cognition, it is more an intuitive act. After about one year, this infant will show concern about another baby's crying and can become quite agitated if it is the crying of a sibling, often attempting to comfort the baby.

As the child develops cognition and language throughout early childhood, she uses words as consolation, and towards the beginning of middle childhood she will begin to consider why another is upset and will try to remove the hurting with soothing talk. Throughout the development of perception and reasoning of middle childhood, as a child develops an understanding of a wider range of emotions, she develops an ability to see the emotions in perspective, within a 'bigger picture'. She begins to develop a social consciousness, and within this consciousness a social conscience. She develops an understanding of distress within a greater view of sickness, poverty, war and natural disaster. She feels within herself what it can be like to be within these social events.

A child's social environment affects her development of empathy. If she grows up in a sensitive environment surrounded by others who also have concern for her, she is more likely to show concern for the sensitivities of others. Parental teaching of kindness and also guidance in how to manage uncomfortable emotions, such as anger and greed, also help the child to respond appropriately to the emotions of others. Growing up in a harsh and punitive environment retards a child's ability to develop an empathetic nature.

There appear to be gender differences in the responses of empathy. As a generalisation, girls tend to show a response of *caring* for others whereas boys tend to feel the *justice or injustice* of a situation. The development of empathy in the middle childhood years is the result of the child recognising a greater range of emotions, not only in themselves but in others, a greater competence in social relationships, particularly outside of their own family group and a greater control of their own emotions through the learning of appropriate expression.

## The development of altruism

Altruism is behaviour that benefits another person without any expected reward for the self. Psychologists call this *prosocial behaviour*. It is intentional and voluntary.

The development of altruistic behaviour begins in early childhood at about the time that a child develops a real interest in playing with other children. She will offer comfort to another child and share a toy with him. As a child develops control over her own emotional behaviour throughout middle childhood and into adolescence, her sharing and caring abilities increase. Conscious awareness is the awareness of self, the self in the present moment and how the self behaves. It is the ability to know and understand our own actions by recognising our past actions, to see our own actions in the present and to have an awareness of our actions *before* we commit them. This is lifelong learning.

## Social Development

A child's sense of self develops as she becomes more independent. Knowing where she 'fits' within her family, within her peer group and then in the wider community enables her to develop healthy social skills. A child's perception of who she is and whether she fits comfortably within different groups allows her to determine her own personal expression, to develop leadership skills and also the ability for character discernment through interaction with other children.

By the age of ten years, a child has informally become a member of her peer group, whether playing sports or sharing a hobby. At this age, a child primarily has same-sex friends and her friends assume greater importance in life. As the child becomes more independent, she relies less on family and more on peers. A child who feels good about herself is better equipped to withstand peer pressure.

Self-perception, through awareness of appearances, is also quite noticeable during the middle years and a child can sometimes express dissatisfaction with how she sees herself. Learning to love our self comes with self-acknowledgement of who we are and with finding love of our self beyond the physical. Loving encouragement within the family is very important because peer criticism can bite hard in the middle years of childhood.

Moral behaviour develops during middle childhood. Moral behaviour comes with an understanding of *right* and *wrong*, and a child's own acceptance and growth of personal responsibility. Moral behaviour is also dependent on the child's development of self-discipline. Children in middle childhood make up their own social rules and these differ from the rules that are acceptable in adulthood. Rules evoke a response of right or wrong. The individual is 'wrong' if she does not stick to the rules of the clan, group or society. So even though moral behaviour is developing in the middle childhood years, it is set within its own paradigm in that the rules of the group can differ from the rules of society.

A child's development of moral behaviour is influenced by the child's understanding of her own world and her internal motivations in relation to her world's cultural demands.

To understand the moral behaviour of this child is to enter her world and its culture. This child is developing a measure of independence, of alliance and loyalty to friends and family and, at the same time, she has a need to push beyond her own family boundaries. Freud called this period of development the *latency stage*, when a child will repress sexual desires in order to concentrate on developing friendships with members of the same sex and developing academic skills. This preference releases the child from the stresses of sexual attraction, which is the tension that arises in their adolescent years.

Moral behaviour is behaviour that is the result of developing a *conscience*. A developed conscience is the source of human values, which are the guiding principles for human behaviour. Morality provides the security that a human being needs for survival within society.

From as early as one year of age, a child's actions communicate her ability to know that his behaviour can create a response within another person. From the age of about nine months she has understood the word 'no'. During her fifth 100-day period she knows well how to say it.

She will engage in unacceptable behaviour, such as biting, kicking or hitting, if this enables her to get what she needs for her survival within her family. This little child does not respond to reason. She does not yet have the brain connections for reasoning. The only way that she and those around her can diffuse this behaviour is through distraction, by guiding her carefully into another activity or into her bed for a nap (tiredness contributes to 'bad' behaviour).

Up until the age of eight years, this is how a child needs to learn to manage her frustrations. She learns that behaviour other people do not like, or that breaks things and that hurts her and other people is *not OK*. She also learns that 'good' behaviour, the behaviour that people like and love her for, is rewarded. She is motivated to obey in order to avoid punishment, to be obedient for its own sake and to be good for the avoidance of trouble or damage. She is still a little child who is dominated by the laws of the 'big people' in her life. Her self-determination is not based on reason; it is based on her innate need for survival.

During the early childhood period of moral behaviour development, the small child learns obedience to rules when they are in her *own* best interest, or in the interest of others so long as this does not create conflict with her own interest. It is an egocentric morality. What she views as 'right' is her definition of fairness, equal exchange, a deal or agreement and her belief that people should be seen to be treated equally.

As a child grows towards her age of reason, she emulates her loved ones, listens to their reason and gradually learns why and how behaviour is either 'good' or 'bad'.

When a child is about nine years old, she begins to develop a new level of moral behaviour – the conventional stage of morality that is learnt through middle childhood and adolescence. This level of moral behaviour is through interpersonal expectation and conformity. The child in middle childhood is beginning to behave in a way that shows her as a 'good person' – she aims to please or help others and to be rewarded for this good' behaviour. She conforms to the stereotyped image of the majority – her peers and the pressure imposed by the peer group. She is learning and accepting the validity of the golden rule of moral behaviour – *do unto others as you would have them do unto you*.

As the child enters adolescence, she begins to believe in the duty to fulfil the agreements and laws of society. Her moral behaviour is based on duty and the social order. It is in adulthood that higher levels of moral behaviour such as the greatest 'good' for the maximum number of people are sought, and the will or rights of the majority are not to be violated. However 'universal' values and rights – for example, the right to life or the right to freedom – are to be upheld regardless of the majority opinion or action.

Seeing a small child develop a conscience that is then reflected in her moral behaviour validates not only the child's development as a worthy citizen but also the parents' example and teaching of moral behaviour. When a child reaches the age of consciousness, at about eight years, she has, through this learning of 'right', 'wrong', 'good' and 'bad', established the foundation upon which higher levels of moral behaviour can be established. She can now advance beyond 'self' to 'group', where she can do for others as she would like them to do for her.

Behaviours that respect the rights and needs of others are essential for the continued existence of human groups and therefore the existence of each individual within those groups.

## INSIGHTFUL MOMENTS

During middle childhood a child is developing greater perception. It becomes a lot easier to reason with her and in turn she is beginning to develop the skills of reasoning with you. She can be quite persuasive! While developing a stronger sense of self, she is still your friend and wants to please you. The rebellion of adolescence is still a way off for she depends a great deal on the closeness and safety of the family group during middle childhood.

When you have identified her intelligence strength, the one that dominates her multiple intelligences, then this can become an abiding source for her. She will feel supported and comforted by your interest in her strength and if she is appropriately encouraged, even though her strength may not be nurtured by her orthodox schooling, she will feel that her family is on her side. This is a good foundation for an easier journey through her adolescent years.

This child is developing insight, a greater sense of responsibility, a feeling for caring and justice, not only for herself and family and friends but also for the wider world. This 'insight" is directly linked to the characteristics of the third eye and the sixth energy centre. She is developing a sense of the bigness of our world.

The middle childhood years are a very good time for children to be given responsibility for raising a pet. This enables them to develop insight and preparation for the parenting roles of their own adulthood, whether they are parenting their own children, the children of their community or the animals that come into their life.

Especially warm moments are evident when a child begins to offer help to peers or family and then waits for the offer to be accepted. She also develops a greater sensitivity to moral behaviour. As this grows, physical aggression between peers tends to mellow. Middle childhood sees a growth in friendly and good-natured chasing and 'fighting' play, which is 'rough and tumble play' rather than aggressive behaviour. This type of sociable physicality seems to come at the end of childhood before children enter puberty and the self-conscious years of adolescence. It is as if the middle childhood years represent the autumn of our growth towards the winter of adolescence, which prepares for the growth of adulthood, the beginning of a higher level of growth cycles.

## Personality and character development

Personality traits are individual and subjective and they vary widely. As personality is subjective we can, for example, have or lack a sense of humour, we can be outgoing or shy, friendly or stoic, and we can develop interests and passions. While basic personality is always within the individual person, it can be improved with exposure to the arts, people, travel, reading, hobbies and adventure and exploration.

Character traits are constant and objective and timeless. Character is a personality pattern. Character can be taught and it can be self-modified. Each individual has the choice to accept or reject character traits. We can also act 'out of character' – we can be seen as a brave person, but then on occasion can perform a cowardly act and be regarded to have 'acted out of character'.

Our moral values and behaviour define our character.

From the age of about eight years, core ethical values begin to form the foundation of a person's character. As we see these values manifest in a child, we can know that the child is on path to being a 'good character'. Seeing this development in a young child is very inspiring.

*Trustworthiness* manifests in honesty – no deceiving, cheating or stealing. It is being reliable, having integrity and doing what we say we'll do. It is having the courage to do the right thing and build a good reputation. It is being loyal – to family, friends and country.

*Respect* manifests in our treatment of others and through living the golden rule of moral behaviour – do no harm. It is about not threatening, hitting or hurting anyone. It is being tolerant of differences whether they be of race or ability. It is having good manners and refraining from 'bad' language. It is having consideration of the feelings of others. It is having dignity and dealing peacefully with anger, insults and disagreements.

*Responsibility* is doing what we are supposed to do. Persevere – keep on trying! It is always doing our best, using self-control. It is being self-disciplined, thinking before we act – considering the consequences of our acts. Personal responsibility is being accountable for our choices in life.

*Fairness* is playing by the rules, taking turns and sharing. It is being open-minded and listening to the points of view of other people. It is about not taking advantage of another person and of not blaming others carelessly.

*Caring* is being kind to all creatures, being compassionate and showing that we care. It is expressing gratitude, forgiving others and helping others in need.

*Citizenship* is doing our share to make our establishment and our community better. It is about cooperating, getting involved in community affairs and staying informed. It is about voting for our leaders, being a good neighbour, obeying laws and rules. It is respecting authority and protecting the environment.

When parents are getting to know their little baby, they are learning about the personality that the baby has brought into the world and which she will enrich in life through involvement in the arts, interacting with people and developing skills through special activities. Image, techniques and skills are part of personality and can have a great influence on outward success.

Personality is the tip of the iceberg – it is the part of us that people first see. Our character lies hidden beneath the surface and manifests itself in our trustworthiness, respect, responsibility, fairness, caring and citizenship.

What parents, families, communities and education bring to the child is the *development of character*. This happens throughout infancy, childhood, adolescence and adulthood and through the power of the self. It is constantly instilled, developed and rehabilitated. When a yacht is sailing into the wind, it is always being corrected to stay on course. Seeing a child 'sailing into the wind' is special. It is seeing the child learning through her mistakes and correcting to wind shifts and the waves or upheavals of life.

True effectiveness and success in life lies in good character.

# PARENTING WITH PERCEPTION, COMMAND AND INSIGHT

Wisdom is the quality or state of properly discerning or judging what is true or right. It is the essence of prudence. Wisdom is the ability to think through the *heart* so that the mind can transcend knowledge. Wisdom is not knowledge – there are many knowledgeable people who do not have wisdom. There are some little children who do not have knowledge but they sometimes have great wisdom. Wisdom comes from within, with perception, command and insight.

True spiritual wisdom grows out of honest self-knowledge, the kind of self-knowledge that develops through knowing who we are as individuals and what we, as individuals, identify with. It also needs the strength of our intuitive processes, our ability to empathise and the courage to trust who we are.

Wisdom demands a willingness to learn and to evolve.

Because wisdom arises out of love rather than logic, the heart needs to be open and trusting. Then the mind can draw on its knowledge to enable wisdom to come forth.

*Wisdom demands honesty and humility.*

*Judgement* is expressed wholly from our own point of view and it denies another person's right to live and express who they are in whatever way they choose. It is a mental and emotional process. Judging another is a means of invalidating that person by setting our self 'above' them, When we enter into judging or criticising another, then we need to ask ourself, 'Why am I judging or criticising this person, why am I feeling threatened, and what part of me am I denying?' 'Why am I denying this person their rights as an individual to have their own opinions and their unique behaviour?'

When we judge something, we compare it to some standard that we have been given by our environment – our family, our school, our peers and the media. When we judge another person, it is our own ego which, under threat, seeks to dominate the other by denying that person's right as an individual.

*Discernment* differs from judgement in that it is the ability to perceive differences between people and between things. It leads to an understanding and acceptance of those differences, rather than the condemnation of judgement.

We often *judge* our children and blame their frailty on their other parent. If we recognise and accept their 'frailty' as a *difference*, then we practise discernment. As we own the truth of our own differences we grow, and through our growing our children can learn discernment and can also understand judgement and where it comes from. Children model themselves on their parents as teachers. Your child is learning from you and will love you for your honesty.

*Ethics* are the principles that define behaviour as right, good and proper. These principles do not always dictate a single moral course of action, but they do provide a means of evaluating and deciding between different options. Ethics is concerned with how a moral person should behave. Values are not ethics – values are the personal inner judgements that determine how a person *actually* behaves.

When we are motivated by self-interest and a pursuit of happiness that denies the rights and happiness of others, we create barriers to living in an ethical manner. Cheating in examinations, lying on resumes and distorting or falsifying facts are not 'ethical' behaviours. The real test of our ethics is whether we are willing to do the right thing even when it is not in our own self-interest.

Acquiring wisdom requires that we live ethically.

When the third eye energy centre is not in balance, it can be the result of over-intellectualising about life. This is an activity of dominant left-brain rationalising through analysing and theorising our life events and a denial of the right-brain ability to 'feel' the emotions of what is going on in our life.

If on the other hand, we live too much in our feelings – an activity of the right side of the brain – then we begin to lack discernment, with a resulting inability to plan our life and set objectives and goals in order to fulfil our dreams and achieve a vision of how we would like our world to be.

When this energy centre is balanced and functional, then intuition becomes a way of discernment and allows wisdom to develop. With this comes a greater insight of life events, an acknowledgement of feelings, the creation of vision and an ability to bring a vision to fruition. We can make our dreams come true.

An ability to cope with change and to flow with the tide brings tranquillity to our existence and an acceptance of whatever life presents us. When we are intuitive we develop an understanding of our 'inner being', and we also develop a very real sense of the abilities and knowing of others, their frailties and their strengths. Our intuition enables us to support them through their difficult times, which are part of their own growth and development, and then, through their growth, the development of their own intuitive abilities.

This is where we can support our children in their spiritual growth – through seeing and experiencing our own. We, as human beings, have an enormous potential for spiritual growth through the getting of wisdom.

Self-realisation is the seeing and accepting of who we are as individuals – what we can see as our own strengths and frailties. It is the search for the truth of who we are.

The first oracle written over the gateway to the temple at Delphi in Greece was *Know Thyself*. This is the process of self-realisation. Having the willingness for self-transformation through growth and change is the first step towards this happening for us. While some define self-realisation as the act of reaching one's full potential, I believe it to be a part of the process of self-actualisation.

*Self-actualisation* is part of our need to reach our full potential. The psychologist Abraham Maslow proposed in his *Theory of Human Motivation* that as human beings meet their basic needs of life survival, they then seek to satisfy successively 'higher needs' such as esteem and actualisation. Our self-esteem centres around how we feel about our *self*. If our self-knowledge is strong and all our basic needs for survival are met or at least partially met, then we can achieve self-actualisation.

Human beings need to engage themselves in activities that give them a sense of contributing to society and also a sense of self-value. These activities can be through our work or in our hobbies and interests. If we do not have this need met then we develop a sense of worthlessness

Maslow defines the personal qualities that can lead to self-actualisation as follows:

- Experience life as a child does, with full absorption and concentration.
- Try something new rather than sticking to secure and safe ways.
- Listen to your own feelings in evaluating experiences rather than to the voice of tradition or authority or the majority.
- Be honest: avoid pretences or 'game playing' (be authentic).
- Be prepared to be unpopular if your views do not coincide with those of most people.
- Assume responsibility.
- Work hard at whatever you decide to do.
- Try to identify your 'defences' and have the courage to give them up.

Maslow studied the characteristics of people whom he considered to be self-actualisers. He found that they perceive reality efficiently and are able to tolerate uncertainty. They accept themselves and others for what they are. They are spontaneous in thought and behaviour. They are interested in solving problems and this often includes the problems of others. They have a good sense of humour, they are highly creative, they appreciate beauty and they are concerned for the welfare of humanity.

Self-actualisers are able to transcend their cultural conditioning to become world citizens. They are capable of deep appreciation of the basic experiences of life; they establish deep, satisfying interpersonal relationships with a few rather than with many people; and they are able to look at life from an objective viewpoint – they are able to discern rather than to judge others. They are authentic – being comfortable with who they are, with what they do in life and with where they are going in their life.

In the striving and attainment of all of these qualities there is spiritual growth. There are periods in our adult life when we reach these qualities and feel strong about our self. There are our private moments when we can feel quite fragile. In these moments too there is spiritual growth. It is all part of being human.

The search for the meaning of life comes through self-realisation and self-actualisation. When we begin to know and understand our purpose in life, we can then set the goals necessary for achieving it. Sometimes this realisation can lead us to a career change or assessing the validity of our relationships or the pursuit of a high endeavour. In this we can find a more mystical, higher meaning of all things

We are intuitive when we listen to and act on our strong inner voice. A mother has great intuition – she can know when her child is in trouble on the other side of the world. Yet often we do not heed our inner knowing part of us.

We exist on many levels. We can see, touch and understand our physical level. We can feel our emotional level. When we rationalise, we are aware of our mental level. But where does the spiritual part of us reside and how does it communicate with not only our own physical, emotional and mental levels but also with the spirit of others? This is the sphere of the Akashic field of the astral plane – the place of our dreams, the phenomena of 'out of body' and near-death experiences, and profound religious and mystical experiences. It defines our connectedness and the interrelationships of all things.

Parenting within the sixth centre of consciousness is nurtured through wisdom. Wisdom is conceived and born through the union of the mind and of the heart. When we open our sight to the wisdom and teaching that our child brings to us and own our humbleness, then we become the teacher that our child needs and desires. All we need is an open mind and a loving heart.

*God rests in reason ...*
*God moves in passion.*

KAHLIL GIBRAN *THE PROPHET*

# SECTION IV
## Self-reflection

# SAHASRARA

## *The Crown Chakra*

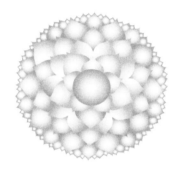

# INTRODUCTION

Sahasrara is unique and stands alone. However, the other chakras cannot function effectively without it, nor it without them. This centre is as mysterious as its associated pineal gland. Many of us only have glimpses of the magnificence of this centre, some of us not until the end of our earthy life span.

We cannot expect a small child to behave and think as a rational and wise person, nor to have the ability to understand the complexity of time and space. If a small child had these abilities, then life would not offer much in the way of fun, experimentation and learning for his eager and exuberant soul, and we, as 'grown-ups' would not have the pleasure of travelling and learning with him. Therefore it is not until a child grows into an adult that the seventh chakra really begins to develop.

The seventh energy centre, Sahasrara, is the centre where we experience unity or connectedness with all things, all people and our Universe. From this centre we can expand beyond self to a concept of a thousand possibilities in the quest for divine wisdom.

This is our centre of prayer, meditation, reflection and spiritual understanding.

Self-reflection illuminates our life history and, like a mirror, shines it back on us. It is through self-reflection that our centre is revealed. It is a form of self-assessment and often it reveals the parts of us with which we have lost contact, the paths from whence we have strayed, and the past that we have denied. Yet it is only in learning through self-reflection that we can maintain our balance, to live our life on purpose and to stay in touch with our own divinity.

Self-reflection, through thought, reveals to us our true self.

# The Seventh Energy Centre

## SAHASRARA
### 'Thousandfold'

## *The Lotus of One Thousand Petals*

### Enlightenment

COLOUR: Violet, is the colour of *unity*, accorded by the Christian church
to signify extreme unction, the sacrament of anointment to a higher order.
It is the colour that indicates an understanding beyond knowledge. Together
with Indigo, the colour associated with our Third Eye, violet stimulates
clairvoyance and psychic ability.

MUSIC: Indian Classical music known as Raga, a melodic improvisation. The
unique essence of a raga is its spiritual quality and its manner of expression and it
is through the years of dedicated practice and discipline under the guidance of his
guru that the artist is able to put 'prana' or the breath of life into his performance.
Ravi Shankar, the great contemporary Indian sitar player, writes: 'The highest aim
of our music is to reveal the essence of the universe it reflects, and the ragas are
among the means by which this essence can be apprehended. Thus through music,
one can reach God.'

PHYSICAL SYSTEM: Cerebral cortex, upper skull

ENDOCRINE GLAND: The pineal gland

SENSE AND TOTEM: The seventh chakra has transcended the physical so has
no correlating sense or totem animal attributed to it.

# SAHASRARA – ENLIGHTENMENT

Sahasrara is a lotus of 1000 petals pointing down, with its seedpod and stem sitting over the uppermost portion of the head like a skullcap. A thousand petals, or 1000 months, represent the mature years of a person's life.

The elemental association of Sahasrara is thought. This is the thought of higher or spiritual consciousness, which connects us to all others and to all things. When we have no self-consciousness, we are at one with the Universe. It is a journey of the soul, not a goal, and it leads to a consciousness that is defined as cosmic or Christ consciousness.

When we commune with nature we are attuned to the spiritual essence of all things. We come to the stillness within us. Higher thought comes in that moment of stillness when we know that we have 'come home'. It is when we *know* that God is within us. Higher thought is when we know that nothing else matters. In fact, there is no matter and no illusion. It just is. When a baby comes into the world, this is the way of his existence. If you ever have the chance to look into the eyes of a fresh newborn in the minutes after birth, then you see God. It is a miraculous and transcending experience.

Sahasrara is associated with the pineal gland, the highest and most mysterious endocrine gland in the body. Situated in the middle of the brain, close to the crown of the head, the pineal gland, in the shape of a tiny pine cone about the size of a pea, consists of two lobes that have fused to become one. It is the only single organ or unit within the brain. All other parts of the brain are paired.

The pineal gland is the least understood gland of the endocrine system, and the only gland not under the direct control of the pituitary gland. It is controlled by the hypothalamus, a very complex part of the brain, which links the nervous and endocrine systems. The hypothalamus coordinates many seasonal and circadian rhythms, complex homeostatic mechanisms and many important stereotyped behaviours and must therefore respond to many different signals, some of which are generated from outside the body. It is as if the hypothalamus is the body's cosmic transfer station for information that reaches us on a subtle level beyond the reach of our ordinary senses.

The hypothalamus is responsive to light: the day length and photoperiod for generating circadian and seasonal rhythms; olfactory (smell) stimuli, including pheromones; steroids, including gonadal steroids and corticosteroids; neurally transmitted information, particularly that which is generated from the heart, the stomach and the reproductive system; autonomic inputs of the involuntary immune system; and blood-born stimuli such as chemicals or hormones, including insulin, pituitary hormones and blood concentrations of glucose.

It is also responsive to stress. The hypothalamus is bounded in part by specialised brain regions that lack an effective blood-brain barrier, which is a barrier that prevents the passage of substances, such as drugs, bilirubin, or toxins, from the blood to the cerebrospinal fluid and brain. The pineal gland also lacks an effective blood-brain barrier and this is why this tiny gland is so vulnerable to environmental substances.

The hypothalamus determines the clear differences in both structure and function of the male and female bodies. The gonads or sex glands release sex steroids that influence the development of the neuroendocrine hypothalamus. They determine the ability of females to exhibit a normal reproductive cycle and of both males and females to display appropriate reproductive behaviours in adult life. From about the seventh week of embryological life, the human testis secretes high levels of testosterone and this determines the male phenotype. It is what makes little boys into little boys. This high level of secretion continues until five or six months after birth, further consolidating the strong sex differences between girl and boy infants.

The action of pheromones aids synchronisation of ovulation so that when females co-habit their menstruation cycles often occur at the same time. Pheromones also influence our sexual behaviour, inviting attraction between the opposite sexes that leads to mating and reproduction, thereby ensuring the continuity of the human race.

Within the hypothalamus is found the suprachiasmatic nucleus (SCN), the generator of circadian (day) rhythms, which regulate many different body functions over a 24-hour period. The suprachiasmatic nucleus receives information of light impulses from the retina of the eye. These nerve impulses descend to the spinal cord and then project to the superior cervical ganglia, a cluster of nerve cell bodies located in the neck near the spine. From there the information is transmitted via nerve fibres to the pineal gland, which, in a process called transduction, converts the nerve signal into a hormonal signal. This process produces the hormone called *melatonin*. Melatonin is unlike other hormones in that it is mostly released into the cerebral spinal fluid. From the cerebral spinal fluid it is then absorbed into the blood stream.

The main functions of the pineal gland are the production of the neurotransmitter serotonin and then its conversion by nerve light impulses into the hormone melatonin. Melatonin is a very powerful antioxidant. Antioxidants are substances that inactivate (and therefore protect the body from) oxygen free radicals, which damage cell membranes, DNA and other cell structures and may cause problems such as heart disease, cancer, Alzheimer's disease, Parkinson's disease, cataracts and rheumatoid arthritis. Antioxidants may also contribute to retarding the ageing process. Melatonin is therefore a very important part of the immune system.

The pineal gland is a rich source of serotonin. Serotonin is the chemical that helps us to maintain a 'happy feeling' by keeping our moods under control. It does this through helping with sleep, calming anxiety and relieving depression.

Serotonin is the body's chemical of wellbeing. It is also believed to co-ordinate our 'biological clock', which is the mechanism within the body that controls our biorhythms, such as eating and sleeping, regardless of external time. Serotonin and melatonin are biogenic amines, which are the simplest hormone molecules produced in the body. Not only is the pineal gland a rich source of serotonin. So too are many plants. The Bodhi tree, beneath which the Buddha was believed to have been sitting when he received enlightenment, is one of those plants.

The functions of the pineal gland remain to this day, mostly undiscovered – it is a part of the human body that still contains a mystery. The 17th-century philosopher Descartes believed that the pineal gland was the 'seat of the soul'.

I believe the pineal gland – also called the epiphysis, from the Greek *epi* meaning higher/outer and *physis*, growth – is the source of higher consciousness and enlightenment, providing a connection with the universal consciousness of all things.

Cerebro-spinal fluid bathes and protects the central nervous system. It 'floats' or supports the brain so that it does not weigh heavily on the spinal cord. It also facilitates the exchange of nutrients necessary for the health and welfare of this delicate nerve tissue. Cerebro-spinal fluid is not static – it is in a constant state of flux, pumped around the brain and spinal cord in a rhythmic pulse. This is known as the cranio-sacral rhythm. Orthodox medicine does not officially recognise this rhythm, even though it is the last rhythm of the physical body to cease after death. Just as the cardiovascular system moves our blood and its molecules of oxygen and carbon dioxide through our arteries, veins and capillaries in a red river of physical life, so does the cranio-sacral system move the precious spinal fluid and its chemical molecules of emotion in a clear river of spiritual life.

The elemental association of Sahasrara is thought. This is not the thought of rational thinking, but the higher thought of contemplation or reflection. It is in the contemplation of *life* that we can find the soul within and come to a kind of peace that transcends our understanding of worldly existence. It is within this space that we can achieve a state of grace that is born out of gratitude. When the soul is nurtured through forgiveness – and this includes *self*-forgiveness – then it is able to become one with all others and with all nature. It is in this state that we have cosmic consciousness. We can attain a state of bliss.

A newborn child has no self-consciousness, he has not yet developed his ego but exists in a state of selflessness, at one with the universe. He is noble, humble and embodying *God*. During his first 100 days on earth, his journey is to become 'earthed' – becoming a member of his tribe and of the bigger world. As he becomes more grounded, he enters his second 100 days when he begins to have a worldview of duality – being separate from others, especially from his mother. When he reaches the developmental stage of the crown energy centre and a higher consciousness in his more mature years, he moves into the experience of unity with all things.

The soul yearns for this unity and it is through Sahasrara, the seventh energy centre, that unity is attained.

# THE EXPERIENCE OF UNITY

We interact with many influential people, parents, friends and teachers throughout our life. When these are true gurus or mentors in life, we learn and grow because the wisdom that a guru is able to impart comes with humility and light. A guru is, literally, one who dispels darkness. He knows *who* he is, and because he has begun to let go of his ego, he is able to bring light into life through imparting wisdom and through teaching the spiritual aspects of existence.

As we absorb a guru's pearls of wisdom and begin to radiate their lustre, we become enlightened. *We see the light*. Wisdom is an experience. It is travelling our own personal journey. Knowing the things that we can change and the things that we cannot change, and having the wisdom to know the difference, we become teachers ourselves. This is the capacity of every human being. And it comes as we let go of our ego.

When we achieve balance in the crown centre, we develop a more positive outlook towards life. Our ego begins to quieten down so that instead of being ruled by the ego's divisiveness, limitations and judgements, we have compassion and acceptance not only for others but also for our own self. When the crown centre is not balanced we live in the realm of the ego and the egotist. The egotist believes that he is separate from, and above others and separate from a universal force greater than himself.

This belief leads him to a conviction that is only through his own striving and effort that he can get anywhere in life. The egotist is proud and arrogant and constantly looking for self-gratification, entrenched in a material world. Deep within, life for an egotist can be fairly dark and miserable.

The egotist's belief that being in control of every aspect of life will lighten this inner darkness drives him to concentrate on the material things of life, to bring achievement and fame to an inner emptiness. The egotist has difficulty in truthfully defining his own identity. He sees emotions as a sign of weakness. The egotist can be very hard on himself and imposes his will on everything he can control.

But perhaps the defining nature of the egotist is his denial of all things spiritual, especially the deep inner spiritual side of himself. When we deny our spirit we separate our self from others, because it is only through spirit that we can become one with another. We talk about a 'kindred spirit' or a 'soul mate'. It is through spirit that we can achieve this kind of closeness. And it is the movement of spirit within us that brings ecstasy in sexual union.

As we come to recognise and accept our ego, we begin to lose our attachment to it.

All those 'bad' things that happened to us way back in our childhood, and in our adult relationships are contained within our ego.

If we cling to those experiences, then they limit us because we become addicted to the *energy* of them. If we view them and accept them as our lessons in life, then the negative energy held within them is released and we can begin to distance ourself from them. The energy of these experiences no longer binds us to them. This is how we can let go of our ego. In the process of letting go we gain serenity and as serenity radiates from us it attracts others to our wisdom. As we impart and share our wisdom we begin to become our own guru, infusing light into our own life. Wisdom does not have needs, nor does it have to belong to the narrow bindings of our life experiences.

When this energy centre is balanced we can access spiritual wisdom, sometimes called enlightenment. This is different from the earthly wisdom of the third eye. Spiritual wisdom enables us to access and reveal our own inner divinity and sacredness.

*The distinction between the grasses and the blossom is the same as between you not knowing that you are a buddha, and the moment you know that you are a buddha. In fact there is no way to be otherwise. Buddha is completely blossomed, fully opened. His lotuses, his petals, have come to a completion ...*
OSHO

# EPILOGUE

## Self-reflection

The formative years of a child's life prepare him for his growth through adolescence and into adulthood. He gradually learns that he is no longer the absolute centre of the universe but simply a part of it, just as all others are.

Sigmund Freud defined the personality as having three functions: the id, the ego and the superego. The id is the function that we are born with. It ensures our survival because it satisfies the needs of the dependent child who wants instant gratification. It satisfies our primitive needs to be fed, to be warm, to be touched and eventually our wants and desires.

During our very early childhood, in our first 500 days, we function in this irrational and emotional part of our mind – the part that looks after our feelings and our needs and desires. This is the role of the id.

Gradually, from about 18 months of age, as we begin to develop some self-control and a view of the real world, the ego starts to develop and to negotiate with the Id in order to keep it in check. Our ego develops through an increasing awareness that in the real world we can't always get what we want.

From about the age of five years we begin to develop an idea of 'right' and 'wrong', and the seeds of our conscience are sown. This is the role of our developing superego.

When we reach the age of eight years, the age of reason and rational thought, the developing mind functions through the id, the ego and the early superego.

As we grow into adulthood we more fully function with the moral part of the mind – all the values that we have learnt from our parents, our schooling and from society in general – that gives us the boundaries for the 'good behaviour' that has been defined by those influences. We have also by now developed a more mature conscience.

Our life drama is the interplay between our id, which is the seat of our impulses, our ego, which negotiates with the id while at the same time pleasing the superego, and our superego, which keeps us on the 'straight and narrow'.

The id, the ego and the superego need to be well balanced in order to have good mental health. When this system is balanced we begin to develop wisdom. This wisdom is a worldly wisdom: we become experienced, wise people within our community, whether this is our family, our workplace or the wider world.

When the psychic system is not in balance, then one of these functions begins to dominate it. If the id is too strong, then behaviour reveals itself in self-gratification with little caring for others. If the ego is too strong, then behaviour can be extremely rational and efficient, but at the same time cold, boring and distant. If the superego is too strong, there develops a feeling of perpetual guilt, while at the same time there may be overbearing saintly and judgemental behaviour towards others. When one aspect is too strong, then the results are deficient in the other aspects. For example, if the id or the ego dominates the system, then the superego will be weak. This can manifest in lower moral values and lack of conscience.

This imbalance can become the conflict of our adult life. In our search for meaning these are the areas that we begin to question, to try to come to terms with and in our earthly wisdom, to recognise and accept in others, and to change within our self. We yearn to have balance of mind so that we can achieve peace and harmony.

It is in this search for balance and our peace of mind that we can have glimpses of the possibilities of our higher 'self', the spiritual guru within. This is the realm of the seventh energy centre Sahasrara, which draws its energy from a wider universe and imparts it to the first six energy centres that have brought us to adulthood and its rational mind, its conscience and its definition of purpose.

This is the rebirth of our spiritual intelligence.

# APPENDICES

# APPENDIX 1

## QUALITIES OF THE CHAKRAS

The system of the chakras is an organised one. These energy centres do not function in isolation, but are interdependant on the functions of each other. However, each energy centre operates at its own level and it may be under- or over-active. For the system to be balanced and to be functioning smoothly, each energy centre or chakra needs to be in a state of balance. Each energy centre is associated with physiological systems within the body.

### THE NEUROENDOCRINE SYSTEM OF THE HUMAN BODY

The nervous system controls homeostasis (balance) through nerve impulses conducted along the nerves. The endocrine system releases its hormones into the blood stream, which then delivers hormones to virtually all cells throughout the body, though only some will use them. The nervous and endocrine systems are coordinated as an interlocking super-system – the neuroendocrine system, which coordinates the functions of all the body systems. Nerve impulses often have their effects within milliseconds. Hormones can have their effect on the body up to a few hours after their release into the blood stream.

### THE ENDOCRINE SYSTEM AND ITS ASSOCIATION WITH THE CHAKRAS

The endocrine glands produce hormones that control many body functions. The pituitary gland, which is situated at the base of the brain, is the master gland, which, under the regulation or command of the hypothalamus, releases hormones that control all the other endocrine glands of the body. The only endocrine gland that is not under the control of the pituitary gland is the pineal gland, which is under the direct control of the hypothalamus.

There are seven main endocrine glands in the human body: the adrenal glands, the gonads (ovaries or testes), the pancreas, the thymus gland, the thyroid gland (with its parathyroid glands), the pituitary gland and the pineal gland. Each chakra is influenced by one of these glands and vice versa.

The endocrine glands develop early in an embryo, because the secretions of these glands are necessary for the development of the baby in the womb as well as just after birth, so that the baby can mature in a healthy way.

Embryological development of the baby is dependent on the beginning growth of the physical body from three types of tissue: ectoderm, mesoderm and endoderm. Each endocrine gland is created from one of these different tissues.

## The Nerve Plexuses Associated with the Chakras

Each of the first five major chakras of the physical body corresponds to the major nerve plexus situated in that area of the body. A plexus is a network of major nerves, such as spinal or cranial nerves, joined with varying numbers of nerve fibres from adjacent nerves. The plexus acts as a relay station for nerves that support different organs of the body.

The first energy centre is located at the base of the spine at the coccygeal plexus, the second is situated in the lower abdomen or sacral plexus, the third is situated in the solar plexus in the upper abdomen, the fourth at the sternum in the cardiac plexus, the fifth in the throat area or pharyngeal plexus. The sixth and seventh energy centres are located within the brain and also have significant nerve tissue centres. The sixth centre, the third eye, is situated near the optic chiasma, which is the crossing point of the optic nerves.

The seventh energy centre at the crown of the head is associated with the pineal gland where sympathetic postganglionic fibres terminate. When light enters the eye and strikes the retina, nerve impulses travel to the suprachiasmic nucleus of the hypothalamus. From here, nerve impulses are transmitted to the superior cervical ganglion. This is how the pineal gland receives nerve impulses of light that enter the eyes.

## YOGA AND THE CHAKRAS

Yoga is a gentle exercise system that benefits both body and spirit and can bring clarity and peace to the mind. Bringing clarity and peace to the mind opens the way to spiritual development. Its gentle exercise routine helps to keep the body supple and youthful by allowing an unobstructed flow of energy through its energy channels..

It is the Hindu tradition that developed the practice of Yoga as a path to peace, health and enlightenment, and raised our awareness and knowledge of our energy centres – chakras.

Yoga is a tradition of teachings and techniques that help the practitioner to understand and aspire to the higher levels of consciousness that rise above the lower levels of consciousness, which deal with our basic needs for survival.

The word 'yoga' means union. The practice of yoga is the science of uniting the body, mind and spirit, and of uniting our individual soul with the universal spirit. Yoga is meditation in motion.

## ACUPUNCTURE AND CHANNELS OF ENERGY

Acupuncture is a therapy based on the principle that there is a nervous connection between the organs of the body and the surface of the body. All living beings contain *Qi* or vital life energy which, ideally, is in a state of perpetual balance within the body and with the environment. Imbalance of this energy, which may be caused by stress, can lead to dysfunction of the body's organs and eventually result in disease. The Qi in the body flows along channels. On each channel there are several acupuncture points. Stimulation of these points (usually with needles) can influence the flow of energy, and the body's functions, to restore the balance. The practice of *medical* acupuncture is also based on understanding of neurophysiology and anatomy.

Acupuncture works on the principle that in all *dis*-ease, whether mental or physical, there are tender areas at certain points on the body, which disappear when the disease is cured. These areas are called acupuncture points. There are about 12000 points, which are joined by unseen energy channels known as meridians.

The Chinese describe how the body's life forces or *Chi* circulate in these meridians and they then interpret all disease as a disturbance of these energy or life forces. Acupuncture is a major part of traditional Chinese medicine and in recent years it has become popular with conventional western medicine.

# LIGHT, COLOUR AND THE CHAKRAS

The chakras have associated qualities, such as colour, element and sound. The qualities of colour cannot be understood without a basic appreciation of the nature of light, which is fundamental for the existence of life.

Light is *visible* energy, which is generated from atoms and subatomic particles through the potential of electromagnetic energy.

Light travels at a speed that cannot be exceeded. This speed is constant at 300 000 metres per second. When light hits the retina at the back of the eye, it is translated into nervous impulses that travel to the part of the brain that interprets them as 'seeing'. Our sense of sight is not possible without light.

Visible light consists of the colours of the spectrum. In the 17th century, Isaac Newton built on the work of the French philosopher René Descartes and discovered how the colour spectrum is produced from light. In a darkened room he placed a glass prism so that a shaft of sunlight shone through it and the light separated into its seven constituent colours – the colours of the rainbow. This discovery forms the basis of our understanding of colour. Newton concluded that light or colour consists of waves, and that each colour has a different wavelength and vibrates at a different frequency.

The colour spectrum is the visible part of the electromagnetic spectrum. There are many other wavelengths that are not visible to the human eye and these are manifest in television waves, radio waves and microwaves, etc.

All matter, including our physical bodies, is sensitive to electromagnetic radiation at all frequencies, even though we are only aware of light or the visible spectrum. Electromagnetic waves do not require a medium in order to transport their energy. They are waves that have an electric and magnetic nature and are capable of travelling through a vacuum. Therefore all things are capable of responding to the electromagnetism of light and to its constituent colour.

Within the human body the seven main energy centres of the Hindu tradition vibrate within the colour spectrum and that is why we are able to attribute different colours to them.

The wavelengths of the energy that can be detected by the human eye extend from about 760 nanometres at the red end of the spectrum to about 380 nanometres at the violet end. The shorter the wavelength, such as violet, then the higher the frequency of the vibration. The human sense of sight registers every little change in wavelength within this band of energy as a different colour. The vibrations of the chakras have been measured and through these measurements corresponding colours have been attributed to them.

The colours that we see and wear affect our moods even though we are often unaware of their effects. The colours at the lower end of the electromagnetic spectrum – red, orange and yellow – radiate energy while those at the higher end – the blues, indigo and violet – absorb energy. Green is the bridging colour, a combination of both yellow (giving or electric energy) and blue (receiving or magnetic energy).

A newborn baby has a very pale and delicate aura, which is filled with very pale colours. Traditionally a new baby is dressed in white, which, because it contains all colours, allows the infant to absorb what he requires. Colours associated with babies were pale, in the belief that a colour such as pale blue calms a restless baby and that pale pink is the colour of unconditional love. Since orthodox hospital treatment of neonatal jaundice uses ultraviolet blue light to help a baby to excrete the jaundice from the body, then we can accept that colour is a powerful influence on all living creatures.

## SOUND AND VIBRATION

Sound is a wave created by vibrating objects; it travels through a medium transporting energy from one location to another. Sound travels through air, water and solid matter by the disturbance of particles that are supported by an elastic element, which some call the ether. The medium is simply a series of interconnected and interacting particles. The original source of the soundwave is a vibrating object, such as the vocal chords of a person, or a musical instrument, or a tuning fork, or a collision of objects that disturbs the first particle of the medium, which then interacts with another particle. This transportation through particle interaction is a mechanical wave. Mechanical waves of sound, unlike the electromagnetic waves of light, require a medium in order to transport their energy from one location to another, and for this reason they cannot travel through regions of space which are devoid of particles. Sound cannot travel through a vacuum.

As a soundwave moves through a medium, each particle of the medium vibrates at the same frequency. If a tuning fork is struck, its vibration can be heard as the particular note for which it has been designed. If there is another tuning fork of the same frequency nearby, then it will absorb the vibration and start to vibrate at the same frequency even though it has not itself been struck.

The amplitude of sound is measured in decibels. The frequency or pitch of sound is measured in hertz. One vibration per second is measured as 1 hertz (Hz). The human ear is capable of detecting soundwaves with a wide range of frequencies, ranging between about 20 Hz to 20 000 Hz.

Any sound that occurs outside of the human range of hearing is known as either infrasound or ultrasound. A frequency below 20 Hz is known as an infrasound. Any sound with a frequency above 20 000 Hz is an ultrasound. The sensations of frequencies are referred to as the pitch of a sound.

Different animal species have unique abilities to detect frequencies. A dolphin can detect frequencies as high as 200 000 Hz. These wonderful creatures have the ability to detect ultrasounds, sounds with a very high pitch that is inaudible to the human ear. The elephant, however, has the ability to detect infrasound (very low pitch sound) because an elephant has an audible range of about 5 to 10 000 Hz.

*Cymatics*, visible sound, or the study of how vibrations, in the broad sense, generate and influence patterns, shapes and moving processes, is a term coined by Swiss physician Dr Hans Jenny in the 1960s. Jenny described the results of experiments he conducted to show what happens when various materials like sand, spores, iron filings, water and viscous substances are placed on vibrating metal plates and membranes.

Drawing on the work of the musician and physicist Ernst Chladni (1756–1827), Hans Jenny was able to photograph the shapes and patterns. Chladni had demonstrated that sound does affect physical matter and that it has the quality of creating geometric patterns.

Jenny was convinced that biological evolution is a result of vibrations; that the nature of those vibrations determined the ultimate outcome and that genes, cells and various structures in the body are influenced by different frequencies.

Each energy centre of the body responds to a unique vibration. That is why the vibration of a particular colour or musical note is denoted to it. The lower the chakra, then the lower the vibration of colour or musical note that is attributed to it. Conversely, the 'higher' the chakra, then the higher the rate of vibration of colour or note.

This demonstrates that sound creates *form* and that it is also linked with vibrations of consciousness. In a world which demands scientific proof for the validation of belief, this is a welcome gift for we can now grasp the healing qualities of music, the destructive forces of noise pollution, the vibration of colours and we also have a greater understanding of resonance, where people who have the same rate of vibration are drawn or attracted to each other.

# THE ELEMENTS

The elements are fundamental materials of which all matter, including our physical body is composed. They are the elementary or basic components of all things. A substance that cannot be broken down or reduced further is, by definition, an element. It is through recognising chemical elements and their symbols that we are able to understand and ultimately control our environment. This is the basis of the atomic elements. However there are five primary elements in the spiritual sense. These are the basic biological 'elements' or elements of nature that are essential for our existence and for an understanding of our existence, and they are the symbols of our life.

These are the elements that are the philosophers' symbols. Aristotle, Socrates, Plato and other early philosophers depended on an understanding of these elements. The ancient elements of nature are earth, water, fire, air and ether. A common question concerning these elements of 'nature' is that if water is known to consist of molecules $H_2O$ (2 parts hydrogen plus 1 part oxygen), and is therefore reducible to the atomic elements of hydrogen and oxygen, then why is water considered to be elemental? It is because water (and air which is made up of nitrogen and oxygen) is recognised as elementary for the survival of all living beings, and so is considered a fundamental element for life.

These natural elements all make up not only the physical parts of us but also the unseen mystical parts of us. The eastern Hindu and ancient Greek philosophies agree that everything in this universe is made up of these five elements.

# Earth

Earth represents the solid state of matter. We can scoop up earth into our hand, feel its texture and sift it through our fingers. We can think of earth as the rocks, the soil, and the solid parts of us as physical beings and of our natural environment.

Earth gives us the 92 known naturally occurring chemical elements (such as Na (sodium) and K (potassium) that are the building blocks we learnt about in school science lessons. We need elements such as these to allow all our body systems to function. Our bones need calcium. Our blood haemoglobin depends on iron. Our nervous system would not function without a proper balance of calcium, potassium, sodium and magnesium.

It is estimated that the human body consists of 60 billion cells – nerve cells, skin cells, blood cells, and so on. Each cell is made up of molecules, each molecule is made up of atoms and each atom is made up of subatomic particles.

The four main chemical elements present in the body are oxygen (O, 65%), carbon (C, 18.5%), hydrogen (H, 9.5%), and nitrogen (N, 3.2%), all of which make up about 96 per cent of our total body mass. The other 3.9 per cent is made up of the elements: calcium, phosphorus, potassium, sulphur, sodium, Chlorine, magnesium, iodine and iron. About 0.1 per cent of our total body mass is made up of trace elements present in minute concentrations: aluminium, boron, chromium, cobalt, copper, fluorine, manganese, molybdenum, selenium, silicon, tin, vanadium and zinc. So it can be seen that our earthy, physical body is composed of elements.

Each one of these elements is made up of atoms, which are the smallest units of matter that enter into chemical reactions. An element is simply a quantity of matter composed of atoms that are all of the same type. Pure coal dust or a diamond are both made up entirely of carbon atoms.

An atom consists of three major types of subatomic particles: neutrons, protons and electrons, the neutrons and the protons making up the nucleus of a cell, and the electrons having a negative electronic charge that enables the atom's energy function for chemical reactions. This is how the cells of the body carry out their functions, such as taking up haemoglobin and transporting oxygen to all the other cells of the body.

# Water

Water, which gives the body fluidity, is an essential part of us. Without water we would be rigid, unable to move, unable to feel and unable to have energy, because water is essential for the conduction of our energy and the flexibility of our flesh.

We come from water. Without the fluid of the womb, we would not learn how to be flexible human beings, and we would not be able to be born. Water facilitates our passage in life and it cushions it. Without moisture, there can only be friction and life then seizes up. If we did not consist of water, we would not be able to breath, to think and to dance.

The human brain consists of 85 per cent water and the human adult body of 70 per cent water. When we start out on our life journey as a fertilised egg we consist of 96 per cent water. At birth a baby consists of 80 per cent water. As adults, we consist of 70 per cent water until we reach the end of our lifespan in old age, when we consist of 50 per cent. When we reach old age we begin to lose our fluidity and therefore our flexibility. It becomes just a little bit more difficult to move and to flow with life.

Amniotic fluid, the fluid that bathes and supports a baby in the womb, consists of water and salts that are very close to the balance of seawater. The salinity of the oceans remains relatively constant at about 3.4 per cent. If this level of salinity were to increase by even the smallest percentage, our life on this planet would be very different. If the salinity increased to about 6 per cent, even for a brief period, all the life in the ocean would be extinguished, and the oceans would be as barren as the Dead Sea.

The sea within us, that 70 per cent of water that we consist of, is dependent on the balance of all the chemical elements present in our bodies.

# Fire

Fire is hot and dry. Fire is the element that makes things happen. It is our body's 'get up and go'. Fire enables our physical body to function through electromagnetic energy. Our respiration, digestion and nervous systems could not function without the energy of fire or, in scientific terms, the energy of chemical reactions. We cease to live when there is no longer energy to drive our heartbeat.

Fire is elementary for creating charge and change, and for our survival on earth. The sun is the cosmic fire that provides us with both heat and light, and is the energy that moves the global atmosphere (air) and thus the pump, which is the prime mover of the life-sustaining water cycle.

*Radiant* energy is energy that travels in waves. The body loses heat by the radiation of heat waves to cooler objects nearby. In this way a room can warm up just by the radiation of heat from the body. In a room at 21 degrees Centigrade, about 60 per cent of heat gain is by radiation in a resting person. Think of how we can warm up our bed or the chair that we are sitting in. If we did not radiate the heat that is formed through our body functions, then we would burn up. We also radiate the unseen energy known as our subtle energy – the energy that consists of our emotional spirit.

*Electrical* energy results from the flow of charged particles. In our body, electrical energy involves the movement of charged particles called ions. Impulses in nerve and muscle cells are examples of electrical energy. Our brain energy is electrical energy. We are able to think with electrical energy.

*Heat* energy is the energy transferred from one thing to another because of a difference in temperature. We are able to warm each other just by holding each other close.

*Chemical* energy is a form of potential energy. When chemicals form or break apart, chemical energy is absorbed or released in the form of radiant heat or electrical energy. When the body is growing and renewing itself, such as for the construction of bones, the growth of hair and nails, the replacement of injured cells, it needs nutrients. As the body cells break down these nutrients, they store chemical energy in a form that can be used for building processes.

*Mechanical* energy is the energy due to either the position or the movement of a mass (body). It may be potential energy if the body is still, or kinetic energy if the body is moving. Many body processes convert chemical energy into mechanical energy to perform movements such as the beating of the heart to pump blood.

*Kundalini* energy is human energy and it is the body's healing energy. It is our emotional energy, the energy that comes from passion, such as love, anger, and enthusiasm. Without the movement of Kundalini energy, the psyche does not grow and flower. Kundalini can be triggered by yoga practices, meditation, physical stimulation such as strenuous exercise or a sudden accident, near-death experiences and by mental excitement. As our chakras or energy centres develop and grow, through kundalini energy they touch each other and therefore stimulate the chakras above and below. This results in an increased rush of energy and awareness throughout our whole system, known as *Kundalini* force.

*Kundalini* energy is symbolised by the caduceus, a sceptre or wand surmounted by a pair of wings and entwined by two serpents. This is the staff of Aesculapius, the Greco-Roman god of medicine, and is still used today by doctors and pharmacists throughout the world as their uniting insignia. The symbol of the caduceus is not unique to Greek mythology, as it has also been found in India, carved on tablets dating from the third millennium BC.

The true power and magic of Hermes, Aesculapius and the Brahmin, symbolised by the caduceus and staff, is the magic and power of the soul. Kundalini is the fire or driving force of the soul and it is only with this spiritual energy that physical healing can take place. Physical healing and spiritual healing are dependent on each other. The healing of one cannot take place without the healing of the other.

Even though fire is a form without substance, it possesses the power to transform the state of any substance. It converts food to fat (to store energy) and to muscles (to motivate us). It creates the impulses of nervous reactions, our feelings and even our thought processes.

# Air

Air is existence without form. It is the primary form of matter. It is also the gaseous form of matter that is mobile and dynamic. Air is a necessary element for fire to burn. Air is a mixture of the elements nitrogen (78% parts) and oxygen (21%) and other gases, which surround the earth and form its dry atmosphere. Within the body, the oxygen, which is absorbed from the 16 kilograms of air that we daily breathe into our lungs, is the basis for all the energy transfer reactions within the body. It is therefore essential for our existence.

When a baby takes his first breath of air it means he is living and independent. With the first breath of air, a baby's sense of smell is activated, so it is also through the breath, that memory is activated. While breath has always been closely linked with the soul, the nature of air is spiritual.

Air is a physical substance, which has weight and is made up of molecules, which are constantly moving. Moving air has a force that will lift kites and balloons up and down. Air is the palpable symbol of *invisible* life, and maybe this is why, of the five elements, it is the most difficult to describe. Air makes most forms of life on earth possible, delivering the oxygen that they need.

# Ether

Ether is the space in which everything happens. The ancient natural elements of the philosophers, earth, water, fire and air are found separately only in two-dimensional systems. To give them cohesion, to be part of a whole, or to be part of a three-dimensional universe, they need to be held within an element that is formless and elastic. This element is known as ether.

The elements are defined by the space that supports them and separates them. The ether defines the many relationships between the different elements. It is the medium in which all things exist and it is inherent in all things. Every cell of us is surrounded and supported by the ether. Within each cell there are atoms that are surrounded and supported by the ether. Within each atom, each subatomic particle is surrounded and supported by the ether. Without the ether, we as human beings would just be jumbled, unsupported, formless piles of particles.

The ether is the quintessential element. Without the ether all other elements would be indefinable. Without the ether there would be nothing to carry soundwaves and without the vibration of soundwaves, there can be no form. The biggest problem for scientists is that nobody had been able to detect and describe the *qualities* of the ether. Albert Einstein, while doubtful of the qualities of the ether, could not dismiss outright the existence of it. In his general theory of relativity, which describes space in terms of gravitational forces that are endowed with physical qualities, he had to accept that there are physical properties of space itself, and that these properties constitute a kind of ether. 'To deny the ether is ultimately to assume that empty space has no physical qualities whatever. The fundamental facts of mechanics do not harmonise with this view … According to the view of the general theory of relativity, space is endowed with physical qualities; in this sense there exists an ether.' Einstein was talking about the gravitational nature of the universe – now described as the 'gravitational field'.

## THE SENSES

The brain has no physical contact with the world. Everything that the brain knows or reacts to comes to it through the senses. There are five senses that enable us as humans to relate to and learn about the environment in which we live.

The five senses were described by the Greek philosopher Aristotle, who believed that the process of gathering knowledge begins with the senses, that repeated sense experience leads to memory and that these senses lead to a form of insight and even to intuition. We are then able to figure out the universal features of things

These five senses – smell, taste, sight, touch and hearing – are dependent on an organ. The organ that we need for the sense of smell is the nose; for taste, the tongue and mouth. Touching depends on the skin, our hearing depends on the ear and our sight is dependent on our eyes.

There are three non-contact senses – sight, hearing and smell – which do not need immediate physical contact with what is being sensed. They rely on a physical medium through which they receive their information.

Sight uses the electromagnetic spectrum, hearing uses waves in air or through water, and smell uses molecules that are carried in a medium such as air or water. The contact senses, touch and taste, need direct contact with what they are sensing.

The sixth sense is the sense that we have for indescribable knowing, the kind of knowing that is at a cellular level of our being. We don't know what the information is, nor from where it comes. It is simply, and profoundly, a deep inner knowing.

Each of the senses are associated with an organ of the body that sends messages to the brain, which in turn processes the message, brings it to conscious awareness and then enables the body to respond to the stimulation of the sense.


# Touch

The first sense to develop in the womb is the sense of touch. The brain processes the sense of touch from nerve impulses from the skin and other parts of the integumentary system.

Touch is not only the ability to touch our self or touch another or touch an object. Touch is also the sensation of the feeling of being touched. We have an innate desire to caress and massage the baby in the womb with long tender movements, which on an energetic level, the baby is aware of. Mothers do it spontaneously, without any prompting or teaching, and often they are unaware that they are doing it. Touch is the fundamental interaction between a baby and her parents. Touch is essential for a baby's physical growth and also for her emotional development.

Our skin is one of the largest organs of the body, both in surface area and in weight. For an average-sized adult, it covers an area of about 2 square meters and weighs about 4.5 to 5 kilograms. Skin, as an organ, is part of the integumentary system, which consists of the skin (epidermis), nails, hair, nerve endings and teeth. All of these are part of the wonderful world of touch.

Our skin is an amazing part of us. It encloses us in a protective bubble, it helps regulate body temperature, it excretes impurities. It also gives off wonderful pheromones to help us attract a mate, helps with immunity, is a blood reservoir and it synthesises vitamin D. But one of its greatest functions is that it allows us to feel. When we talk of our feelings, we are talking about our emotions.

Skin is forming on the embryo at the end of the fourth week after conception. By the end of seven weeks it consists of three layers. By 17 weeks epidermal ridges have formed on the palms of the hands, including the fingertips, and the soles of the feet and toes. These ridges constitute our fingerprint – the part of us that proves our physical uniqueness; and this little baby in the womb is not yet five months in the making.

The sense of touch is also an internal sense. We can feel when parts of our body are not comfortable. We may have indigestion or a headache, because the nerve endings where those feelings of discomfort are send messages to the brain, which sorts them into the type of feelings that they are.

In the same way, if there is something on our skin, say a mosquito biting, then the brain enables a response, such as brushing away the irritation, and sometimes without us consciously realising it.

# Hearing

The sense of hearing is a non-contact sense, in that is does not rely on direct contact with the origin of sound but rather on soundwaves. The sense of hearing enables us be part of humanity in an intimate way through the development of language.

For most humans, hearing is their second most important sense. It is known that a restless babe in the womb quietens to soothing words spoken by his mother or to music and that he responds to angry sounds with anxious movements and raised heartbeat.

All the senses support each other and responsiveness to sound provides support for a young baby's visual and tactile exploration of the environment.

The ear consists of three sections: the internal ear, the middle ear and the outer ear, which is the part that is visible at the side of the head. The inner ear is the first of the divisions of the ear to appear in the embryo, early in the fourth week. This is followed by the beginning development of the middle ear and at six weeks the external ear becomes evident.

Fibres of the sound-receiving system (the 'acoustic analyser') begin to myelinate or mature six months after conception, completing this process very gradually until the child is about four years of age. This myelination or nerve insulation, which permits sound transmission signals, enables hearing in a baby weeks before birth.

Our hearing gives us a social connection with others. If a baby is able to hear while in the womb, then he is already learning about his environment and his relationships. The mother's heartbeat and tummy gurgles, the muffled sounds from the outside world, and the music of life are already influencing and stimulating his senses.

# Sight

The sense of sight has ensured the survival of the human species. Without sight, humans would have been unable to hunt for and to gather their food. We depend on the sense of vision more than any other sense for active exploration of our environment. Seventy per cent of the body's sense receptors are found in the eyes.

The sense of sight is one of the non-contact senses – it relies on the electromagnetic spectrum and the process of light transmission. The eye gathers light but not all of it is used for outer sight. It is now known that 20 per cent of light that enters the eye passes on beyond it into the brain to enable the hypothalamus and the pituitary and pineal glands to carry out their functions. Vision gathers more information in far less time than any of our other senses.

Formation of the eye begins in the embryo at about 22 days after conception. By day 44, eyelids begin to form and they meet and adhere during the tenth week and remain adherent until the foetus is 26 weeks.

The size of a newborn baby's eyes is about two-thirds of the size of the adult but the nerve connections are not complete so the development of visual acuity is slow. The eyes grow fairly rapidly during the first year after birth, and then this growth begins to slow down into adulthood.

A baby in the womb responds to bright lights; however, the sense of sight is the weakest at birth and does not develop adult competence until a child is about two years old.

# Smell

The sense of smell develops early in the embryo, and it is activated with a baby's first breath. This sense is a chemical sense, is well developed at birth and this is when a baby begins to bond with his parents, particularly his mother.

The olfactory region of the brain is one of the first parts of the embryo's brain to develop. The nose itself develops with the face but at seven weeks the nasal cavity joins the oral cavity at the back of the throat and the olfactory nerve fibres are present. By 12 weeks the olfactory nerves of the foetus are in place between the roof of the nose and the olfactory bulb of the brain. The foetus now has the ability to smell and, as a baby makes breathing movements in the womb, the smells of the amniotic fluid are his first.

This primitive region of the cortex of the brain is a part of the limbic system and includes some of the amygdaloid body. This is considered the primary olfactory area, where conscious awareness of smells begins. Connections to other limbic system regions and the hypothalamus probably account for our emotional and memory-evoked responses to odours. The limbic system of the brain governs the emotional aspects of our behaviour.

Events that cause a strong emotional response are remembered much more efficiently than those that do not. The limbic system of the brain is associated with pleasure and pain, and it is also because it has a primary function in other emotions, such as anger, rage, fear, sorrow, sexual feelings, docility and affection, that it is sometimes called the 'emotional' brain. This is where sexual excitement upon smelling a certain perfume is generated or a smell-evoked memory flashback to a childhood experience arises. The sense of smell is evocative and is closely related to the memories that are laid down in life, particularly in childhood, when it is at its peak.

## Taste

The fifth sense, taste, is manifest with the sense of smell, and is 75 per cent reliant on it. At around the fourth week (28 days after conception) of embryological development, the tongue begins to develop and at about 54 days the tongue develops papillae, which soon develop taste buds. Taste buds are also formed in other areas of the mouth – the palate, the pharynx and the tonsils. A baby in the womb swallows amniotic fluid, the fluid that surrounds him. This may be his first taste of life.

The human adult has about 10 000 taste buds, and a baby's mouth has more. We taste sweet things at the tip of the tongue, sour things at the sides, salty things over the surface mainly at the front and bitter things at the back of the tongue. The human has a low tolerance for bitter-tasting substances.

Very premature babies of 26 to 28 weeks gestation are able to show facial responses to bitter-tasting substances because the reflex pathways between taste buds and facial muscles are established by this stage. The taste buds are functioning well before this. Our responses to bitter-tasting substances can be life-saving defences – most poisonous chemical substances are bitter tasting. We acquire different 'tastes' as we grow older.

The sense of taste is a provocative one – it stirs us, arouses us and it also alerts us. Food is our physical sustenance. If a food is unsafe for us, then often our sense of taste can alert us. Food is part of our social wellbeing – to break bread with others can engage us in communion with them. Food is also very sensual, and is often part of the dance of attraction between friends and lovers.

## MUSIC AND ITS ELEMENTS

This book draws on the characteristics of colour and music. Both are created by wavelength and frequencies – the eye is capable of conveying different frequencies to the brain where they are interpreted as different colours, the ear receives the frequencies of sound before transferring them to the brain for interpretation. While the eye is only capable of receiving the frequencies within one octave, the ear is able to distinguish between tones over about ten octaves. As the brain is capable of receiving vibrations before the sense organs do, our perceptions are formed as the result of resonance and cosmic vibration. This is how music (and colour) can affect us physically, emotionally, mentally and spiritually on a deep biological level.

Music is universal and ancient. There is not a known culture that has not had music imbedded within it. Music is a means of communication not only for humans but also for birds and whales. The use of drumming as a warning system for ancient tribes, the war cry, the lullaby for the sleepless baby, the hymn of praise, and the harmonies and melodies of classical music move us deeply. Music can also be used as a means of enhancing learning as well as for healing and for pleasure.

Melody gives music its 'soul' with its succession of single notes imposing continuity on disjointed sounds; harmony gives music its congruity through consistency and order and the blending or combination of its notes and chords. Rhythm gives music its pattern and structure with regular or irregular pulses. Music is also held within the intervals or silent spaces between the notes and chords. These spaces are the background within which the music is contained. These silences or pauses contain the *essence* of music.

Music has a profound effect on our consciousness. Like a hologram, the microcosm (person) reflects the macrocosm (our environment), and any vibrations that come from without continue to reverberate within us, forming and shaping us as individuals and the way that we are in the world. Music can also *transform* us and so this is a question to consider: can a culture be created and perhaps destroyed by the music it follows? We cannot ignore music because we are so strongly influenced by it.

Not only can music uplift us and transform us, it has a great capacity to heal us. Many health institutions now have music therapists who work with specific types of music to enable physical, mental and emotional healing.

# THE SYMBOLS

A symbol is a means of revealing and conveying an idea across time, across the ages of humans, and across cultures. It is derived from the Greek word *symbolon,* which means a mark, token or ticket. A symbol wakens our imagination through wordless thought, and is something much bigger than its form because it embraces abstract thought and places it in an effective context. A symbol can be used as metaphor to describe the indescribable. The use of symbols is basic to the human mind. It is fundamental to thinking. All religions have their symbols so that followers can grasp the meanings of their beliefs.

The language of symbols is universal. It is common to all humankind, regardless of their culture, race or mother tongue. It is the language of life in all its forms. Symbols link the inner human to the outer world, thereby providing a sense of connection. Sometimes a symbol requires interpretation: it may not be immediately obvious. However, it is through the process of interpretation that humans can have insight.

It is through exploring the symbols of our dreams and meditation that we can journey into our inner psychological and spiritual world. We tend to be drawn to symbols because of an intuitive awareness of the part that they play in our inner lives, and the way in which they resonate with our emotions.

Our ability as humans to use symbols allows us to explore the relationships between ideas, things, concepts and qualities, far beyond the mundane.

## THE MYTHS

A myth is a symbolic tale, and through the telling of it, the myth is able to convey an idea in a form that brings life and clarity to a similar situation. Myths have grown from many different traditions and their beauty and strength are that they maintain their relativity over vast periods of time and, through translation, they carry across cultures. They are universal.

A myth attempts to explain how the world was created or why the world is the way that it is. Myths are stories, which in ancient cultures, were handed down through the oral tradition from generation to generation, until they were written down in a literary form. Often they were recounted in religious scripts, the book of Genesis being one example. The book of Genesis recounts tales of the creation of the universe, earth and of humankind.

We still use these ancient myths to explain current phenomena. Although a myth is no longer specific to a particular culture, there is still a sense that myth is communal, while the symbol can often be private or personal.

When we refer to the Oedipus complex we are referring to the unresolved desire of a child for sexual gratification through the parent of the opposite sex, and the feelings of dislike and jealousy of the child for the parent of his or her own sex. The term 'Oedipus complex' becomes the symbol that is used to shortcut to the Greek story of Oedipus who fell in love with his mother and slew his father.

Once we know and understand myths, we are able to think of our own psyche as we recall the significance of an ancient myth. This helps us to understand a situation and to describe ourselves in relation to that situation.

In Jungian psychology, myths are symbolic journeys through life.

Stories from ancient mythology through to those of modern history have been used in this book to bring clarity to the limitations of our language and for greater understanding of what may appear to be a complex idea.

We live in a contemporary world of myths and they are being re-created in the modern media of film and television. Often we find in the characters of a movie our own reflections or archetypes, and they are quite revealing because we are able to identify with them. Through them and the stories that contain them, we are able to validate ourselves and to validate the situations that affect our life. They also offer us the opportunity to work our way through the issues of life.

# Archetypes

Archetypes are the reflections of the characters who have appeared in the myths and legends and fairytales throughout the ages. These characters represent the heroes and villains who have appeared in these stories, such as the heroic prince in *Cinderella* or the villainous wicked witch in *Hansel and Gretel*.

Archetypes are mirrors of all the emotional qualities that are contained in the nature of being human – the positive and negative aspects of our way of being, our strengths and weaknesses, our loves and hates, our courage and fear. We can heal aspects of ourself by recognising and owning these parts of our own self, and then by aspiring to develop the positive parts of our nature and recognise when the negative parts of our nature begin to manifest in our behaviour.

Carl Jung believed that myths are the symbolic representations of archetypes that mirror the depths of every human mind. Thus the stories, legends and myths of a culture can reveal the archetypes of character structure. Inscribed on one of the gates of Delphi is the edict *Know thyself*. This we can do by consciously witnessing and honestly recognising our own archetypes.

# APPENDIX II

## HUMAN LANGUAGE AND ITS DEVELOPMENT

Language has four components, all of which need to be mastered in order for a child to become skilled in verbal communication: the sounds of language, the meaning of language, the overall structure of language and, finally, the everyday use of language.

The first component, the sounds of language, is known as *phonology*, which is the collection of sounds unique to a particular language. Newborn babies are especially sensitive to the pitch range of the human voice and find speech more pleasing than other sounds. Within the first few days after birth, an infant is particularly attuned to the voice of his mother.

By six months of age, babies, though still unable to talk, begin to organise speech into the sound categories of their family's native language. In the second half of their first year, babies focus on larger speech units that are necessary for making sense of what they hear, until at about nine months they can respond to their own name and can understand simple words.

When we talk to an infant we tend to naturally use 'baby talk' or 'motherese'. This way of speaking to a baby – short sentences with high-pitched, exaggerated intonation, clear pronunciation, and distinct pauses between speech segments – is innate.

From birth onwards, babies prefer to listen to 'motherese' more than they do to other kinds of adult talk. When they hear it they respond with calm visual focus and, as they get older, with their own vocal responses that are similar in pitch and intonation.

The second component of language is *semantics*, which is concerned with understanding the *meaning* of words and word combinations.

When young children first use a word, it often does not mean the same thing as it does to an adult. For instance they may refer to a dog as a 'woof-woof'. At first, parents tend to accommodate this by using the same words, but as children reach the preschool years, they will spend some time learning and applying the right word to its meaning.

When a child has begun to master his vocabulary, he begins to combine words and to modify them. This process comes with the learning of grammar.

*Grammar*, the third component of language, consists of two main parts: *syntax* which is the set of rules by which words are arranged into sentences; and *morphology* which is the use of grammatical 'markers' that indicate number, tense, case, person, gender, active or passive voice and other meanings. In English the addition of a 's' can turn a single word into a plural word, or it can indicate the present tense.

The fourth component of language is *pragmatics*, which refers to the communicative side of language. To be a successful communicator, a child must acquire certain interaction rituals, such as verbal greetings. Pragmatics is the social side of language

Phonology, semantics, grammar and pragmatics are all interdependent. Acquisition of each component helps with the mastery of the other components.

Speech and language normally develop rapidly during the first few years of life and depend on the ability to hear.

The ear consists of three anatomical parts: the external ear, the middle ear and the inner ear. The inner ear is the first of the ear divisions to appear in the embryo and this development begins early in its fourth week. By the 30th week of gestation, the peripheral auditory structures are nearly completely developed and the foetus responds to loud sounds with movement and changes in heart rate.

During the first four weeks after birth of a term baby, there continues to be major structural changes in the hearing pathways of the brain. These changes continue to happen into childhood.

A newborn baby responds to various aspects of the acoustic (sound) world and these responses are diversified, such as the primitive moro or startle reflex. As the baby becomes even more aware of the sounds in his environment, he begins to respond in different ways.

We can identify his quieting behaviour in response to a soothing voice or music, or his ability in localising a sound in his environment by turning his head towards it, and his attention in response to a sound with his ability to consciously focus on the sound and where it is coming from. This is necessary for speech and language development.

If a baby has hearing impairment, then his speech and language development will be slow and challenging for him. This has a profound impact on his social interactions and he will need a lot of loving care and attention to gain these skills. This is why hearing checks are performed very soon after birth and throughout early childhood.

Children develop their speech and language skills in predictable stages. If there is deviation from this pattern of development, it is often a sign that the child has a hearing loss.

This pattern of development is as follows:

**Newborn stage** (0–1 month) when a baby has reflexive behaviour such as startling; sucking and swallowing patterns. He communicates audibly with his crying and he makes vegetative sounds such as grunting.

**Cooing stage** (2–3 months), when a baby develops definite 'stops' and 'starts' in oral (mouth) movement and sound making.

**Babbling stage** (4–6 months), when a baby has greater independent control of his tongue. He makes prolonged strings of sounds, and he experiments with sounds and makes sounds in response to others.

**Reduplication babbling** (6–10 months), when a baby can produce repetitive syllables, he has increased lip control (such as blowing raspberries) and he can utter incompletely formed plosives (p, b, t, d) and make nasal sounds.

**First words** (11–14 months) when an infant can elevate the tip of his tongue, he babbles in a complex way. If a baby at this age is tongue-tied then this stage of speech can take longer to develop.

From birth to five months, a baby begins to react to loud sounds, he will turn his head toward a sound source and he will begin to watch your face when you speak to him. After he has begun to smile, he will begin to vocalise pleasure and displeasure sounds with laughs, giggles, cries or grunts. He begins to make noise in 'conversation' with another.

From six to 11 months of age he will begin to understand 'no-no', he will begin to babble, by uttering connected syllables such as 'ba-ba-ba' or 'ma-ma-ma'. He begins to communicate by actions or gestures such as pointing.

From about 12 to 18 months of age a toddler develops an ability to answer simple questions nonverbally by pointing to objects, pictures, and family members.

At 18 months he uses six to 20 or more recognisable words. He *understands* many more words, and he will try to imitate simple words.

At about two years of age, a toddler has a vocabulary of about 50 words, can understand many more, and he comprehends simple verbs such as 'eat' and 'sleep'. He correctly pronounces most vowels and the consonants n, m, p, h, especially at the beginning of syllables and short words. He also begins to use other speech sounds.

The acquisition of language is one of the most amazing and necessary achievements in life. It allows for phenomenal learning and it enables social development and interaction.

# APPENDIX III

## MEDITATION

Meditation is a word that encompasses many different techniques aimed at achieving a state of peace, enlightenment or ecstasy. It is a means to bring peace to a troubled, busy mind and relaxation to a stressed and aching body.

The mind is always busy. Just for two minutes, try to have no thought or internal chatter and you can discover that it is surprisingly difficult to command the mind to be still and quiet. Meditation aims to quieten this chatter of the *conscious* mind in order to allow revelation of the *subconscious* mind.

During the practice of meditation it is known that the physical body is altered. Blood pressure is lowered, breathing and heart rates slow and digestion calms.

Sometimes a state of ecstasy is experienced. In meditation we just *are*, and the body seems to breathe thankful relief.

The best way to begin meditating is to find a master who can lead you. There are many organisations or groups that can teach one of many methods, including the Transcendental Movement (TM); some Christian organisations; Buddhist or other eastern groups; personal growth organisations and many community education colleges. It is also taught through health organisations and hospitals.

Research has revealed that the area of the brain that is connected to the experience of unity in meditation and prayer is the area that is responsive to our senses. Our senses keep us grounded, oriented in our own surroundings. It is through our senses that we learn about our physical world and are able to navigate our self through it. Our senses ensure our survival in the illusion of our personal surroundings, constantly sending messages to the brain for our safety.

When does the physical world invade our inner safety? This is a personal experience and cannot be defined in general. We, as sensitive human beings, know when our personal space is being invaded, or when we are endangered, or when we are walking into objects and generally being clumsy, such as when we are unable to manage a physical action in relationship to our surroundings. The part of the brain where all these processes are synthesised is believed to be in the posterior, upper parietal lobe. This area is also the part of the brain where there is an increased activity during meditation or prayer and is believed to be the 'God' spot of our brain.

Meditation can also be achieved through exercise or movement such as dance. The whirling of mystical Sufis lifts them into spiritual realms, spinning and spinning into altered states of consciousness until they fall and lie, connected, belly to ground. Children all over the world do this quite naturally, spinning with arms outstretched until they fall quite naturally in an altered state to be one with the earth.

# Bibliography and Resources

The following texts have helped, over time, to shape my world and my words. There are many other worthy resources that you can draw on, including media interviews, articles and the world wide webb.

Atkinson, R.L., *et al.*, *Introduction to Psychology*, 11th Edition, 1993, Harcourt Brace Jovanovich College Publishers, Florida.

Becker, R.O., Seldon, G., *The Body Electric,* 1987, William Morrow, New York.

Bee, H., Boyd, D., *Lifespan Development,* 3rd Edition, 2002, Allyn and Bacon, Boston, USA.

Bentov, Itzak, *Stalking the Wild Pendulum,* 1988, Destiny Books, Vermont, USA.

Berk, Laura E., *Child Development,* 4th Edition, 1989, Allyn and Bacon, Massachusetts, USA.

Brazelton, T. B., *Touchpoints,* 1996, Transworld, Sydney.

Campbell, E., Brennan, J.H., *Dictionary of Mind, Body and Spirit,* 1994, Aquarian Press, London.

Capra, F., *The Tao of Physics,* 3rd Edition, Flamingo, London.

Capra, F., *The Web of Life,* 1997, Flamingo, London.

Cash, Adam, *Psychology for Dummies,* 2002, Hungry Minds Inc., USA

Charlish, A., *Your Natural Baby,* 1996, Eddison-Sadd Editions, London.

Chetwynd, T., *A Dictionary of symbols,* 1982, Paladin Grafton Books, London.

Coghill, R., *The Healing Energies of Light,* 2000, Gaia Books Limited, London.

Cooper J.C., *An Illustrated Encyclopaedia of Traditional* Symbols, 1982, Thames and Hudson, London.

Creager, J.G., *Human Anatomy and Physiology,* 1983, Wadsworth Publishing Company, California.

De Saint-Exupery, A., *The Little Prince* ((Howard, R., trans.), 2000, Harcourt Inc., Orlando, Florida.

Duncan Baird Publishers, *The Complete Dictionary of Symbols*, 2004, Duncan Baird Publishers Ltd., London.

Emoto, Masaru, *The Hidden Messages in Water*, Beyond Words Publishing Inc., Oregan.

Fontana D., *The Secret Language of Symbols*, 2001, Duncan Baird Publishers, London.

Friedman, R.L., *The Healing Power of the Drum*, 2000, White Cliffs Media, Reno, NV.

Gheerbrant, A., *A Dictionary of Symbols*, 1994, Penguin Books, London.

Gerber, R., *Vibrational Medicine*, 2001, Bear and Company, Rochester, Vermont.

Gimbell, T., *Colour Healing*, 2001, Gaia Books Limited, London.

Hachette Livre, *Dictionary of Symbols, Myths and Legends*, 2000, Hatchett Illustrated UK.

Harrison, G.A. *et al.*, *Human Biology*, 2nd Edition, 1983, Oxford University Press, Oxford.

Hazrat Inayat Khan, *The Mysticism of Sound and Music*, 1996, Shambhala, Boston and London.

Heller, J., Henkin, W.A., *Bodywise*, 1991, Wingbow Press, California.

HH Dalai Lama, Cutler, H.C., *The Art of Happiness, A Handbook for Living*, 2000, Hodder Headline, Sydney.

HH Dalai Lama, *The Universe in a Single Atom*, 2005, Little, Brown, London.

Hunt, V.V., *Infinite Mind*, 1996, Malibu Publishing Co., California.

Jenny, Hans, *Cymatics: A Study of Wave Phenomena and Vibration*, 2001, MACROmedia Publishing Newmarket, USA.

Judith, A., *Eastern Body, Western Mind*, 1996, Celestial Arts Publishing, California.

Judith, A., *Wheels of Life*, 2002, Llewellyn Publications, Minnesota, USA.

Judith, A., *The Truth About Chakras*, 2000, Llewellyn Publications, USA.

Jung, C.J., *Man and His Symbols*, 1968, Dell Publishing, USA.

Jung, C.J., *The Archetypes and the Collective Unconscious, 2ⁿᵈ Ed.,* 1969, Princeton University Press.

Kurtz, E., Ketcham, K., *The Spirituality of Imperfection,* 1994, Bantam Books, New York.

Leadbeater, C.W., *The Chakras,* 1985, Quest Books, USA.

Ledoux, J., *The Emotional Brain,* 2004, Phoenix, London.

Levey, J., Levey, M., *Living in Balance,* 1998, MJF Books, New York.

MacKonochie, A., *The Complete Guide to Baby's First Year,* 2002, Anness Publishing Limited, London.

Moore, K. L., *The Developing Human,* 3ʳᵈ Edition, 1982, W.B. Saunders Company, Philadelphia A.

Motoyama, H., *Theories of the Chakras: Bridge to Higher Consciousness,* 1981, Quest: The Theosophical Publishing House, Wheaton, USA.

National Geographic Society, 1998, *Incredible Voyage: Exploring the Human Body,* Washington, D.C.

Newberg, A, D'Auili, E., Rause, V., *Why God Won't Go Away,* 2001, Ballantyne Books, New York.

Norris, S., *Secrets of Colour Healing,* 2001, Dorling Kindersley, London.

Olivier, S., *What Should I Feed My Baby?* 1998, Weidenfeld & Nicholson, London.

Osho, *The ABC of Enlightenment,* 2003, Element, HarperCollins London.

Ozaniec, N., *Chakras: A Beginner's Guide,* 1999, Hodder & Stoughton, London.

Paramahansa Yogananda, *Autobiography of a Yogi,* 1996, Rider Books, London.

Pert, C.B., *Molecules of Emotion,* 1997, Scribner, New York.

Restak, R., *Mysteries of the Mind,* 2000, National Geographic Society.

Segaller, S, Berger, M., *Jung: The Wisdom of the Dream, 1989,* Peribo, Australia.

Sheridan, M.D., *From Birth to Five Years, Children's Developmental Progress,* 3ʳᵈ Edition, Australian Council for Educational Research, Melbourne.

Simpson, L., *The Book of Chakra Healing,* 1999, Sterling Books, London.

Simpson, S., *Chakras For Starters,* 2002, Crystal Clarity Publishers, Nevada.

Stephenson-Meere M., *Baby's First 100 Days,* 2001, Doubleday, Sydney.

Tame, D., *Beethoven and the Spiritual Path,* 1994, Quest Books, USA.

Tame, D., *The Secret Power of Music,* 1984, Destiny Books, Rochester, USA

Tanner, J.M*., Foetus into Man: Physical Growth from Conception to Maturity,* 1990, Harvard University Press, Boston.

The Chiara College of Metaphysics, *Metaphysics Certificate Resource Notes,* 2002, Sydney.

Tortora, G. J., and Grabowski, S. R., *Principles of Anatomy and Physiology,* 8th Edition, 1996, HarperCollins New York.

Upledger, J.E., *A Brain is Born,* 1996, North Atlantic Books, California.

Vulliamy, D.G., *The Newborn Child,* 5th Edition, 1982, Churchill Livingstone, New York.

Wauters A., *Chakras and their Archetypes,* 1999, The Crossing Press, California.

Wauters, A., *The Book of Chakras,* 2002, Quarto Publishing, London.

Whitney, E.N., and Rolfes, S.R., *Understanding Nutririon,* 7th Edition, 1996, West Publishing Company, Minneapolis.

# Acknowledgements

A book like this comes from a long lifetime of learning from others, not only friends and acquaintances but also loved ones. A reflection on my unique inadequacies has shown me the gift of them and the realisation that I did the best I could with the knowledge that I had at the time. This is particularly true of my years of being a mother, so I thank my children for their honesty, their patience and their amazing and continuing love for me. I am still learning from them, and also from my grandchildren who do not hold back either!

I have been greatly influenced by the teachers of my more traditional learning. The wisdoms of John Upledger of the Upledger Institute, Joseph Heller, the creator of Hellerwork postural counselling, Russell Doherty of Chiara College of Metaphysics; and all the teachers and facilitators of PeopleKnowhow (Zoeros Integral Learning) have helped me to develop a new way of thinking and of living.

My orthodox education and professional working life, first as a general nurse and midwife and in later years as an early childhood and family health practitioner, have given me years of contact with willing and generous people who may never have realised just how much they imparted to me. They enabled my mindfulness that 'we teach best what we most need to learn'.

Parenting is the most noble of professions and I am grateful to all the parents who trustingly opened their hearts and minds to me.

Lisa Hanrahan of Rockpool Publishing, with patience has brought this book to life, supported by its editor, Gabiann Marin. I also thank Liz Seymour who has given this book its visual beauty.

Jan Cornall, mentor extraordinaire, showed me how to reach deep inside myself to find my words and to put them together in my own way. She also counselled me well how to 'let go'.

Wendy Le Page (Bryant), niece, friend and very talented speech pathologist, taught me much about life, speech and education.

The special love of, and for, my partner Gary Lewin, who held my hand and travelled with this book from the moment of its inception, is unbounded by time and distance. My appreciation of him, his wise counsel, and his quiet acceptance of things unknown, is beyond measure.

Thank you.